ABOUT THINGS THAT MATTER

SKILL DEVELOPMENT

Emotional Intelligence That Matters

The 24-Hour Miracle That Matters

Happiness That Matters

From Stressful to Successful

A SELF-IMPROVEMENT SERIES FOR SUCCESS

From Bestselling Author

JC Ryan

Emotional Intelligence That Matters
MASTERING EMOTIONS FOR PERSONAL AND SOCIAL SUCCESS

About Things That Matter
A SELF-IMPROVEMENT SERIES FOR SUCCESS

Book 5

JC Ryan

Copyright

Copyright © 2025 JC Ryan

All rights reserved. No part of this publication may be reproduced, distributed, or transmitted in any form or by any means, including photocopying, recording, or other electronic or mechanical methods, without the prior written permission of the publisher, except in the case of brief quotations embodied in critical reviews and certain other noncommercial uses permitted by copyright law.

Your Gift

As a way of saying thanks for your purchase, I'm offering you the first book in the series **About Things That Matter** as a gift.

This book is exclusive to my readers. You will not find this book anywhere else.

You're invited to pause, reflect, and reconsider what truly defines a meaningful life. In a world conditioned to chase money, status, and material achievements, this book challenges the conventional yardsticks of success. Through incisive insight and refreshing authenticity, it guides readers to shift their focus from external validation to the internal foundations that cultivate real fulfillment, purpose, and enduring happiness. It's a call to eliminate distractions, clarify values, and build a life anchored in what matters most.

Visit this link to download your free copy of About Things That Matter or type this address into your browser https://BookHip.com/HLAJBFP

Introduction

I first met JC Ryan some years ago when, as publisher, I interviewed him for Books & Pieces Magazine. We hit it off and became friends. Through his health issues at the time, and the changes he made to his life for the better, we came to discuss this extensive body of work he created, which detailed his journey and served as a blueprint for anyone wanting to improve their lives, both personally and professionally.

Thus came "About Things That Matter," a comprehensive 12-book series that can completely transform your thinking and your successes.

JC wanted my help in putting it all together, and we decided the best way was to offer a series of email courses to complement the books. And to really get it kick-started, JC decided to offer the first course, "Change That Matters," totally free to participants.

Having seen the entirety of this series, I can attest to its robust nature and that it truly is a solid plan for anyone wishing to better their lives, whether personally or in business.

The books and the course(s) have been designed to be followed easily at your own pace and include many additional resources that can be downloaded.

If you've found yourself asking the question: "Is there nothing more I can do with my life?" then this series is definitely for you. It is "About Things That Matter."

Yours in health,

William Gensburger
Publisher & Author
Books & Pieces Magazine (bnpmag.com)
B&P Books (bnpbooks.com)

In Every Life, It's The Things That Matter That Count

About Things That Matter

The Complete Transformation Series

Your Science-Based Roadmap to a Life of Meaning, Momentum, and Purposeful Living

Most people drift through life reacting to circumstances instead of creating them. They work hard but not strategically. They set goals but struggle to achieve them. They want deeper relationships but don't know how to build them. They feel busy but not fulfilled.

What if there was a better way?

The **About Things That Matter** series is your research-backed, implementation-focused system for transforming intention into achievement and dreams into reality. Based on decades of psychological research and tested by thousands of high achievers, this series provides the specific tools, strategies, and mindsets that separate those who merely wish for better lives from those who actually create them:

The complete "About Things That Matter" series provides a comprehensive, science-based system for transforming every area of your life while reclaiming the fundamental human capacities that have become luxuries in our modern world.

Each book builds on the previous ones, creating a compound effect of growth and transformation. You don't need to read them in order, but starting with your biggest challenge area will create the most immediate impact.

The Research Foundation:

- Harvard's 80-year Grant Study on human flourishing
- Stanford's research on the growth mindset and achievement
- MIT's findings on habit formation and behavioral change
- Decades of organizational psychology research on high performance

Foundation Building

Book 1: Change That Matters
Stop Drifting. Start Directing.

Master the psychology of lasting personal transformation through 8 proven principles that turn intention into achievement.

What You'll Gain:
- The neuroscience-based principles that make change stick
- A systematic approach to breaking limiting patterns
- Proven strategies for overcoming resistance and fear
- The mindset shifts that accelerate personal growth

Readers report feeling more in control of their lives within the first week of implementation.

Book 2: Goals That Matter
Turn Dreams into Done.

Create and achieve meaningful goals through purpose-driven planning that delivers real fulfillment, not just external success.

What You'll Gain:
- The SMART goals framework increases achievement rates by 42%
- How to align goals with your deepest values for sustained motivation
- Systems for maintaining momentum through obstacles and setbacks
- The art of celebrating progress to fuel continued success

Goal completion rates increase by 65% when shared with others using these methods.

Book 3: Time That Matters
Make Every Moment Count.

Transform your relationship with time through proven systems that create freedom, focus, and alignment with what matters most.

What You'll Gain:
- The 80/20 principle applied to daily and weekly planning
- Energy management strategies that multiply your effective working hours
- Digital tools and analog systems that enhance rather than distract

- The art of saying "no" to create space for what matters most

Users gain an average of 8-12 productive hours per week within 30 days.

Book 4: Relationships That Matter
Build Your Social Wealth.

Create deep, meaningful connections through authentic communication and relationship skills that enrich every area of your life.

What You'll Gain:
- The five essential relationship roles that every successful person needs
- Communication skills that transform surface connections into deep bonds
- Digital relationship strategies for authentic connection in a virtual world
- Community-building skills that create belonging and mutual support

Noticeable improvements in relationship quality and communication effectiveness within the first conversations.

Skill Development

Book 5: Emotional Intelligence That Matters
Feel Deeply, Respond Wisely.

Master the art of understanding and managing emotions to enhance relationships, decision-making, and personal effectiveness.

What You'll Gain:
- Advanced emotional awareness and regulation techniques
- Skills to read and respond to others' emotions effectively
- Tools for transforming emotional triggers into growth opportunities
- Leadership abilities rooted in emotional wisdom

Improved emotional responses and relationship dynamics within days of applying core techniques.

Book 6: Happiness That Matters
Choose Joy, Create Fulfillment.

Discover the science of sustainable happiness and build daily practices that create lasting contentment independent of circumstances.

What You'll Gain:
- Evidence-based strategies for cultivating genuine happiness
- Tools to break free from comparison and external validation
- Gratitude and mindfulness practices that rewire your brain for joy
- How to find meaning and purpose in everyday moments

Measurable improvements in mood and life satisfaction within two weeks of consistent practice.

Book 7: The 24-Hour Miracle That Matters
Transform Your Day, Transform Your Life.

Design perfect days that compound into an extraordinary life through intentional morning, work, and evening routines.

What You'll Gain:
- Hour-by-hour blueprints for days that energize rather than drain
- Morning routines that set you up for success and clarity
- Evening practices that restore and prepare you for tomorrow
- Weekend rhythms that rejuvenate and reconnect you to purpose

Dramatic improvements in energy, focus, and life satisfaction within one week of implementation.

Book 8: From Stressful to Successful
Stress Less, Achieve More.

Transform stress from a life-draining force into a success-driving advantage through proven resilience and performance strategies.

What You'll Gain:
- Stress reframing techniques that turn pressure into performance fuel
- Resilience-building practices for bouncing back from any setback
- Peak performance strategies used by top athletes and executives
- Recovery and restoration methods that prevent burnout
- Significant reduction in stress levels and improved performance under pressure within days.

Advanced Integration

Book 9: The Connection Code
Crack the Code to Meaningful Relationships.

One-line Summary: Master advanced relationship dynamics, conflict resolution, and influence techniques that create lasting bonds and positive impact.

What You'll Gain:
- Advanced empathy and emotional attunement skills
- Conflict transformation strategies that strengthen rather than damage relationships
- Influence and persuasion techniques rooted in genuine care
- Leadership approaches that inspire and unite rather than divide

Enhanced ability to navigate difficult conversations and deepen existing relationships immediately.

Book 10: Procrastination
Stop Putting Off Your Potential.

Overcome procrastination forever through understanding its root causes and implementing systems that make action inevitable.

What You'll Gain:
- The psychology behind procrastination and how to interrupt the cycle
- Environmental design strategies that make good choices automatic
- Motivation techniques that work even when you don't feel like it
- Completion systems that turn started projects into finished successes

Immediate breakthrough on stuck projects and tasks that have been delayed for weeks or months.

Book 11: Self-Esteem That Matters
Build Unshakable Confidence from the Inside Out.

Develop authentic self-worth through proven strategies that transform self-doubt into genuine confidence and self-respect.

What You'll Gain:
- Tools to overcome negative self-talk and limiting beliefs
- Habits that reinforce your sense of worth daily

- Assertiveness skills to express needs and set boundaries
- The ripple effect of healthy self-esteem on relationships

Noticeable shifts in self-talk and confidence levels within the first week of practice.

Book 12: Thoughts That Matter
Your Brain Is Not Your Boss.

Harness the neuroscience of conscious living to master your mind, emotions, and purpose through proven mental training protocols.

What You'll Gain:
- How to rewire your brain for resilience, clarity, and growth
- Digital detox strategies to reclaim your attention
- Emotional intelligence tools for wise decision-making
- Daily practices to align thoughts with purpose

Mental clarity and emotional regulation improve within days of implementing the core exercises.

Table Of Contents

Copyright 3
Your Gift 3
Introduction 4
About Things That Matter 5
Table Of Contents 11
PART 1 – EMOTIONAL INTELLIGENCE THAT MATTERS 14
About Emotional Intelligence That Matters... 15
Chapter 1: What Is Emotional Intelligence?.. 18
Chapter 2: The Foundation 27
Chapter 3: Self-Regulation.. 34
Chapter 4: Motivation 38
Chapter 5: Empathy 42
Chapter 6: Social Skills 46
Chapter 7: EQ in Action 50
Chapter 8: EQ, Success, and the Things That Matter... 54
Chapter 9: Your 30-Day Emotional Intelligence Challenge 57
Appendices & Resources 61
Bibliography 65
PART 2 – HAPPINESS THAT MATTERS.. 67
About This Book 69
Chapter 1 – Rethinking Happiness 71
Chapter 2 – The Foundations of Lasting Happiness... 77
Chapter 3 – Habits That Build Happiness 84
Chapter 4 – Mindset Shifts for a Happier Life 92
Chapter 5 – Overcoming Obstacles: When Happiness Feels Out of Reach 100
Chapter 6 – Designing a Life that Supports Happiness 108
Chapter 7 – The Ripple Effect 112

Chapter 8 – The 30-Day Happiness Challenge 119

Appendices & Resources 130

Final Reflection & Series Roadmap 141

Bibliography 146

PART 3 – THE 24-HOUR MIRACLE THAT MATTERS 148

About This Book 150

Preface 151

Prologue: The Midnight Realization 153

1. The Gift of 24 Hours 155

2. Beyond the To-Do List 157

3. Start Small, Stay Realistic 159

4. Work Isn't Your Whole Life 162

5. Leisure That Nourishes 165

6. Self-Compassion and Flexibility 168

7. Focus in a Distracted World 171

8. Daily Self-Check-In 174

9. Feed Your Curiosity 177

10. Nothing in Life is Humdrum 180

11. Serious Reading 183

12. Dangers to Avoid 186

Epilogue: The Gentle Revolution 189

PART 4 – FROM STRESSFUL TO SUCCESSFUL 192

Disclaimer 194

Warning 194

About This Book 195

Introduction: The Journey 196

Chapter 1: What Is Stress—And Why Does It Matter? 197

Chapter 2: Mapping Your Unique Stress Profile 201

Chapter 3: The Hidden Costs of Stress 212

Chapter 4: How Stress Can Help You Grow 217
Chapter 5: The Four Pathways to Success 219
Chapter 6: Calming the Mind and Body.. 222
Chapter 7: Designing a Supportive Lifestyle 224
Chapter 8: Eating for Energy and Resilience 226
Chapter 9: Supplements and Herbal Allies... 228
Chapter 10: Mastering Your Mindset.. 231
Chapter 11: Habits That Matter 233
Chapter 12: The Power of Connection 234
Chapter 13: Navigating Setbacks and Change 236
Chapter 14: Celebrating Progress, Not Perfection 237
Conclusion: Living a Life That Matters... 238
Bibliography 239
Your Gift 240
About JC Ryan... 241
Also by JC Ryan... 242

PART 1 – EMOTIONAL INTELLIGENCE THAT MATTERS

To those who understand that emotional mastery is the foundation of all meaningful achievement, and to everyone brave enough to look within themselves to create positive change in their relationships and communities

"If your emotional abilities aren't in hand, if you don't have self-awareness, if you are not able to manage your distressing emotions, if you can't have empathy and have effective relationships, then no matter how smart you are, you are not going to get very far."

— Daniel Goleman

About Emotional Intelligence That Matters

How to Use This Guide for Maximum Impact

- *Emotional Intelligence That Matters* is designed as both a comprehensive learning resource and a practical implementation guide. Unlike books that simply provide information, this guide is structured to help you systematically develop emotional intelligence skills through understanding, practice, and integration.

The Learning Framework

Each chapter follows a proven learning framework:

- **Understand**: Clear explanations of concepts grounded in research but presented in accessible, practical terms
- **Reflect**: Thought-provoking questions designed to help you examine your current patterns and identify areas for growth
- **Practice**: Specific exercises and techniques you can implement immediately in your daily life
- **Apply**: Real-world scenarios and examples showing how to use these skills in various contexts
- **Integrate**: Connections to other areas of personal development and the broader *About Things That Matter* series

Reading Recommendations

- **For Comprehensive Development**: Read the book sequentially from beginning to end, completing all reflection questions and action steps before moving to the next chapter.
- **For Targeted Improvement**: Use the assessment tools in Chapter 1 to identify your strongest and weakest areas, then focus on the most relevant chapters.
- **For Quick Reference**: Each chapter is designed to stand alone, allowing you to revisit specific topics as needed.
- **For Group Study**: Discussion questions and group exercises are included for book clubs, teams, or learning groups.

Essential Tools and Resources

Throughout the book, you'll find:

- **Assessment worksheets** to evaluate your current emotional intelligence level
- **Tracking templates** to monitor your progress over time
- **Practice exercises** for developing specific skills

- **Habit-building guides** for sustainable change
- **Troubleshooting tips** for common challenges
- **Integration strategies** connecting EQ to other life areas

The 30-Day Challenge

Chapter 9 presents a comprehensive 30-day emotional intelligence challenge designed to help you systematically practice all five pillars of EQ. This challenge can be:

- Completed after reading the entire book for comprehensive skill development
- **Used as a refresher** to maintain and strengthen existing skills
- Adapted for specific focus areas based on your individual needs
- **Repeated multiple times** as your skills develop and deepen

Making It Personal

Emotional intelligence is deeply personal. Your emotional patterns, triggers, and responses are unique to your experiences, personality, and circumstances. As you work through this book:

- **Be honest with yourself** about your current strengths and challenges
- **Practice self-compassion** when you notice areas that need improvement
- **Celebrate small wins** as you develop new skills and awareness
- **Adapt the strategies** to fit your specific situation and learning style
- **Be patient with the process**—emotional intelligence develops over time through consistent practice

Beyond Individual Development

While this book focuses on personal emotional intelligence development, remember that EQ is inherently social. Your emotional intelligence affects everyone around you and contributes to the emotional climate of your family, workplace, and community.

Consider how you might:

- **Share insights** with family members or colleagues
- **Model emotional intelligence** in your daily interactions
- **Create emotionally intelligent environments** in your sphere of influence
- **Support others** in their own emotional development journey

Continuing Your Journey

Emotional intelligence development doesn't end with this book. The appendices provide resources for continued learning, including:

- **Recommended books** for deeper exploration of specific topics

- **Online communities** for ongoing support and learning
- Professional development opportunities for advanced skill building
- **Assessment tools** for periodic evaluation of your progress

A Note on Implementation

Reading about emotional intelligence is valuable, but transformation happens through practice. As you progress through this book, resist the temptation to simply consume information. Instead:

- Complete the reflection questions honestly and thoroughly
- **Try the exercises** even if they feel uncomfortable at first
- **Apply the concepts** in your daily interactions
- **Track your progress** using the provided tools
- **Seek feedback** from trusted friends or colleagues about changes they notice

Remember, developing emotional intelligence is not about becoming perfect—it's about becoming more aware, more skilled, and more intentional in how you understand and manage emotions in yourself and others.

Your journey toward greater emotional intelligence starts now. Each page you turn, each exercise you complete, and each insight you gain brings you closer to mastering these essential life skills that will transform your relationships, your effectiveness, and your overall satisfaction with life.

The investment you make in developing emotional intelligence will pay dividends in every area of your life for years to come. Let's begin this transformative journey together.

Chapter 1: What Is Emotional Intelligence?

THE FOUNDATION OF ALL SUCCESS

In a world that has long celebrated intellectual prowess and technical expertise, we've overlooked one of the most critical factors determining success, happiness, and fulfillment: emotional intelligence. You might be the smartest person in the room, possess impressive credentials, or demonstrate remarkable technical skills, yet if you struggle to understand your own emotions, manage stress effectively, connect authentically with others, or navigate complex social dynamics, you'll find yourself hitting invisible barriers that no amount of traditional intelligence can break through.

This isn't a personal failing—it's a gap in our understanding of what truly drives human success and satisfaction. Research consistently shows that emotional intelligence (EQ) is a better predictor of success in virtually every area of life than IQ alone. Yet most of us have never been taught these crucial skills that form the foundation of meaningful achievement and lasting relationships.

Understanding Emotional Intelligence

Defining EQ Beyond IQ: What Emotional Intelligence Really Means

Emotional intelligence is fundamentally different from the cognitive intelligence measured by IQ tests. While IQ reflects your ability to process information, solve problems, and think analytically, EQ represents your ability to recognize, understand, and manage emotions—both your own and those of others. It's the bridge between thinking and feeling, allowing you to make decisions that honor both logic and human nature.

At its core, emotional intelligence is about awareness and choice. It's the capacity to pause between an emotional trigger and your response, creating space for conscious decision-making rather than automatic reactions. This seemingly simple ability—to observe your emotions without being controlled by them—is what separates those who thrive from those who merely survive in our complex, relationship-driven world.

Unlike IQ, which remains relatively fixed throughout life, emotional intelligence can be developed and strengthened at any age. This neuroplasticity of emotional skills means that regardless of your starting point, you can build the emotional competencies that will transform your personal and professional life.

The Five Core Pillars: Building Blocks of Emotional Mastery

Emotional intelligence rests on five interconnected pillars, each building upon the others to create a comprehensive framework for emotional mastery:

1. **Self-Awareness** is the foundation—your ability to recognize and understand your emotions as they occur. This includes knowing your emotional triggers, understanding your patterns, and recognizing how your emotions affect your thoughts and behavior. Without self-awareness, all other emotional skills remain inaccessible.
2. **Self-Regulation** involves managing your emotions skillfully rather than being controlled by them. This isn't about suppressing feelings but about choosing your responses consciously. Self-regulated individuals can remain calm under pressure, adapt to change, and maintain their composure during challenging situations.
3. **Motivation** in the EQ context refers to your ability to harness emotions to fuel goal achievement and personal growth. Emotionally intelligent people are driven by intrinsic motivation—they pursue goals for the satisfaction of accomplishment rather than external rewards alone.
4. **Empathy** is your capacity to understand and share the feelings of others. It's the skill that allows you to step into someone else's emotional world, see situations from their perspective, and respond with appropriate sensitivity and care.
5. **Social Skills** represent the culmination of all other EQ competencies—your ability to manage relationships, communicate effectively, resolve conflicts, and influence others in positive ways. These skills enable you to build networks, lead teams, and create the collaborative relationships essential for success.

The Science Behind EQ: Neuroplasticity and Emotional Learning

Modern neuroscience has revealed that emotional intelligence literally reshapes your brain. Through neuroplasticity—the brain's ability to form new neural connections throughout life—practicing emotional skills strengthens the neural pathways associated with emotional regulation, empathy, and social awareness.

Research using brain imaging technology shows that people with higher emotional intelligence have stronger connections between their emotional centers (like the amygdala) and their prefrontal cortex, the brain region responsible for executive functions like decision-making and impulse control. This biological foundation explains why emotionally intelligent people can remain calm under pressure and make better decisions during stressful situations.

The implications are profound: every time you practice emotional awareness, choose a thoughtful response over an automatic reaction, or empathize with another person's perspective, you're literally rewiring your brain for greater emotional intelligence. This biological reality means that EQ development isn't just about learning concepts—it's about creating lasting changes in how your brain processes and responds to emotional information.

Debunking Common Myths About Emotional Intelligence

Several misconceptions about emotional intelligence can hinder your development of these crucial skills:

Myth: EQ is just about "being nice"

Reality: Emotional intelligence includes the ability to have difficult conversations, set boundaries, and address conflicts directly. Sometimes the most emotionally intelligent response is to be firm or even confrontational when the situation demands it.

Myth: You're either born with EQ or you're not

Reality: While some people may have natural advantages in emotional sensitivity, emotional intelligence is largely learned. The skills can be developed through practice, feedback, and conscious effort at any stage of life.

Myth: Emotions should be controlled or suppressed

Reality: Healthy emotional intelligence involves experiencing and processing emotions fully while choosing your responses consciously. Suppressing emotions often leads to increased stress, anxiety, and relationship problems.

Myth: EQ is less important than technical skills

Reality: While technical competence is necessary, research consistently shows that EQ becomes increasingly important as you advance in your career and take on leadership responsibilities.

The Lifelong Impact of Emotional Intelligence

Personal Success: The EQ Advantage in Life Satisfaction

Emotional intelligence profoundly affects every aspect of your personal life. People with higher EQ report greater life satisfaction, stronger resilience in the face of challenges, and a deeper sense of purpose and meaning. They're better at managing stress, recovering from setbacks, and maintaining optimism during difficult times.

This isn't just subjective experience—it's measurable. Studies tracking individuals over decades show that those with higher emotional intelligence in their twenties were more likely to achieve their personal goals, maintain stable relationships, and report higher levels of happiness and fulfillment later in life. The ability to understand and manage emotions creates a positive feedback loop: better emotional skills lead to better relationships and outcomes, which in turn reinforce emotional well-being.

Professional Excellence: Why Employers Value EQ Over IQ

In today's collaborative, fast-paced work environment, emotional intelligence has become the differentiating factor between good employees and great leaders. Research by the Center for Creative Leadership found that 75% of careers are derailed for reasons related to emotional incompetence, while only 25% fail due to technical incompetence.

Employers increasingly recognize that while technical skills can be taught relatively quickly, emotional intelligence skills—like the ability to work well with others, adapt to change, and maintain composure under pressure—are more difficult to develop and therefore more valuable. This is particularly true in leadership roles, where the ability to inspire, motivate, and guide others becomes paramount.

Companies with emotionally intelligent leadership show higher employee engagement, lower turnover, better customer satisfaction, and improved financial performance. The ripple effects of EQ extend throughout organizations, creating cultures of trust, innovation, and collaboration.

Relationship Quality: The Direct Correlation with Connection

Perhaps nowhere is emotional intelligence more visible than in the quality of your relationships. People with higher EQ have more satisfying marriages, stronger friendships, and better relationships with their children. They're skilled at reading emotional cues, responding appropriately to others' needs, and navigating the complex dynamics that arise in all human connections.

Emotional intelligence enables you to build trust quickly, resolve conflicts constructively, and maintain relationships through challenging times. It's the foundation of intimacy—the ability to be vulnerable, empathetic, and authentic with others. Without these skills, relationships remain superficial or become sources of stress rather than support.

Mental Health: Protection Against Anxiety and Depression
Emotional intelligence serves as a protective factor against mental health challenges. People with higher EQ are less likely to experience chronic anxiety, depression, or stress-related disorders. This protection comes from several sources: better stress management skills, stronger social support networks, more effective coping strategies, and a greater sense of control over their emotional lives.

When challenges do arise, emotionally intelligent individuals are better equipped to seek help, process difficult emotions, and maintain perspective. They understand that emotions are temporary and manageable rather than overwhelming forces beyond their control.

The Cost of Low Emotional Intelligence

Warning Signs: Recognizing Emotional Immaturity
Low emotional intelligence manifests in predictable patterns that can significantly impact your life and relationships. Common warning signs include:
- Frequent emotional outbursts or inability to remain calm during stress
- Difficulty reading social cues or understanding others' emotional states
- Tendency to blame others rather than taking responsibility for your role in conflicts
- Rigid thinking patterns and resistance to feedback or different perspectives
- Impulsive decision-making without considering emotional consequences
- Chronic relationship problems with similar patterns across different relationships

These patterns often develop as coping mechanisms during childhood or stressful periods but become limiting factors in adult life. Recognizing these signs is the first step toward developing greater emotional intelligence.

Relationship Breakdown: How Poor EQ Destroys Connections
Low emotional intelligence is one of the primary causes of relationship failure, both personal and professional. When you can't understand your own emotions or respond appropriately to others', relationships become sources of conflict rather than support.

In romantic relationships, poor EQ manifests as inability to communicate needs effectively, difficulty resolving conflicts, and lack of empathy for your partner's perspective. In friendships, it appears as self-centeredness, emotional volatility, or inability to provide support during difficult times. At work, low EQ shows up as poor teamwork, difficulty with authority, and inability to navigate office politics constructively.

The cumulative effect is isolation and missed opportunities for meaningful connection. People with low EQ often find themselves wondering why relationships don't work out, unaware of their role in creating the patterns they experience.

Career Limitations: Why Technical Skills Aren't Enough

In today's workplace, technical competence is merely the entry fee—emotional intelligence determines how far you'll advance. Employees with low EQ often hit career plateaus because they struggle with the interpersonal aspects of leadership and collaboration.

Common career limitations include:
- Inability to lead teams effectively due to poor communication and empathy skills
- Difficulty adapting to change and helping others navigate transitions
- Poor conflict resolution abilities that escalate rather than resolve workplace tensions
- Lack of influence and persuasion skills needed for senior roles
- Inability to build strategic relationships essential for career advancement

As you move up in any organization, your success becomes increasingly dependent on your ability to work through others, inspire teams, and navigate complex interpersonal dynamics—all emotional intelligence competencies.

Personal Suffering: The Internal Cost of Emotional Mismanagement

Perhaps the greatest cost of low emotional intelligence is the internal suffering it creates. When you can't understand or manage your emotions effectively, life becomes a series of reactive responses to external circumstances. This reactive living leads to:

- Chronic stress and anxiety from feeling out of control
- Depression and hopelessness when relationships and goals consistently fail
- Low self-esteem from repeated interpersonal failures
- Substance abuse or other addictive behaviors as coping mechanisms
- Physical health problems related to chronic stress and poor emotional regulation

The tragedy is that this suffering is largely preventable through the development of emotional intelligence skills. Unlike many life challenges, emotional intelligence is entirely within your control to develop and improve.

Reflection Questions

Take time to honestly consider these questions, perhaps writing your responses in a journal:

How do emotions currently shape your daily life and decisions?

Notice the role emotions play in your choices, from small daily decisions to major life changes. Are you aware of your emotional states as they occur, or do you often feel surprised by your reactions?

What emotional patterns do you notice in your relationships?

Look for recurring themes in your interactions with family, friends, and colleagues. Do you tend to withdraw during conflict? Become defensive when criticized? Struggle to express your needs clearly?

Where has low EQ cost you opportunities or relationships?

Reflect honestly on times when emotional reactions or poor interpersonal skills may have damaged relationships or limited your success. What patterns do you notice?

Action Steps

Complete the comprehensive EQ self-assessment

Use the assessment tool provided in the appendices to evaluate your current emotional intelligence across all five pillars. Be honest in your responses—this baseline will guide your development efforts.

Identify your strongest and weakest emotional intelligence areas

Based on your assessment and reflection, determine which EQ competencies come naturally to you and which need the most development. Most people have uneven profiles, with clear strengths and growth areas.

Set specific EQ development goals aligned with your life priorities

Choose 1-2 emotional intelligence areas to focus on initially, connecting them to your broader life goals. For example, if you want to advance in your career, you might focus on developing empathy and social skills. If you want to improve your marriage, self-awareness and emotional regulation might be priorities.

Remember, emotional intelligence is not a destination but a lifelong journey of growth and development. Every step you take toward greater emotional awareness and skill creates positive ripple effects throughout your life, improving not just your own experience but also the lives of everyone around you.

The foundation you build in understanding emotional intelligence will support all the specific skills and strategies covered in the following chapters. Like the sculptor who could see the horse within the granite block, developing emotional intelligence allows you to see and create the life you truly want—one built on authentic connections, conscious choices, and meaningful achievement.

Questions and Answers From Students And Possible Solutions

1. How do emotions currently shape your daily life and decisions?

- **Daily Decisions**: I often find that my mood influences what I eat or how I interact with others. For instance, when I'm feeling upbeat, I'm more likely to socialize and try new things, whereas a bad mood might lead me to stay home and avoid plans.
- **Awareness of Emotional States**: I generally notice when I'm feeling anxious or excited, but sometimes I'm surprised by my reactions, especially in stressful situations. For example, I might react defensively to constructive criticism without realizing it until later.
- **Major Life Changes**: Emotions play a significant role in major decisions, like career changes. When I feel passionate about an opportunity, I tend to pursue it more vigorously compared to when I feel indifferent.

Solutions:

- **Practice Mindfulness:** Engage in mindfulness exercises, such as meditation or deep breathing, to increase your awareness of emotional states as they occur. This helps in recognizing your feelings before they influence decisions.
- **Journaling:** Keep a daily journal to track your emotions and decision-making. Reflect on how your feelings affected your choices and identify patterns over time.
- **Set Intentions:** At the beginning of each day, set clear intentions regarding how you want to respond emotionally to challenges. This can help guide your reactions.

2. What emotional patterns do you notice in your relationships?

- **Conflict Response**: In conflicts, I often withdraw instead of addressing issues directly. This pattern has led to unresolved tensions in some relationships.
- **Defensiveness**: I tend to become defensive when receiving feedback, which can create barriers in communication with colleagues or friends.
- **Expressing Needs**: I struggle to articulate my needs, leading to frustration in my relationships. I often assume others should understand my feelings without me having to explain.

Solutions:
- **Communication Skills Training:** Participate in workshops or courses focused on improving communication skills. Learning techniques for expressing needs can help address misunderstandings.
- **Role-Playing:** Practice role-playing scenarios with a trusted friend to develop responses to conflict or feedback. This can help you become more comfortable with confrontation.
- **Seek Feedback:** Regularly ask for feedback from close friends or colleagues about your communication style and emotional responses. Use this to gain insight and improve your interactions.

3. Where has low EQ cost you opportunities or relationships?
- **Missed Opportunities:** There have been job opportunities I didn't pursue because I let my fear of rejection cloud my judgment. My inability to network effectively has also limited my professional growth.
- **Damaged Relationships:** I recall a friendship that deteriorated because I didn't communicate my feelings about a misunderstanding. My emotional reactions pushed the other person away, rather than fostering understanding.
- **Patterns Noticed:** A recurring theme is my tendency to avoid confrontation. This has resulted in unresolved issues, which often escalate over time, causing further strain in relationships.

Solutions:
- **Emotional Intelligence Workshops:** Attend workshops focused on developing emotional intelligence. These can offer tools for managing emotions and improving interpersonal skills.
- **Reflect and Analyze:** After a missed opportunity or relationship strain, take time to reflect on what went wrong. Identify specific emotional reactions that contributed and consider how different responses could have changed the outcome.
- **Practice Assertiveness:** Work on assertiveness techniques to express your thoughts and feelings clearly and respectfully. Start with small interactions and gradually build up to more significant conversations.

By implementing these solutions and steps, you can enhance your emotional awareness, improve your relationships, and seize opportunities more effectively.

Chapter 2: The Foundation

SELF-AWARENESS. KNOWING YOURSELF TO TRANSFORM YOURSELF

Self-awareness is the cornerstone of emotional intelligence and the foundation upon which all personal growth is built. Without understanding who you are, what drives you, and how you respond to the world around you, any attempt at change becomes like trying to navigate without a compass. This chapter will guide you through developing the deep self-knowledge that makes lasting transformation possible.

The Root of All Personal Growth

Why Self-Awareness Matters

Self-awareness is not merely knowing your favorite color or preferred coffee order. It's the profound understanding of your emotional patterns, triggers, values, strengths, and limitations. It's the ability to observe yourself objectively, as if you were watching someone else, and to recognize the gap between who you are now and who you want to become.

Research consistently shows that self-aware individuals are more confident, make better decisions, communicate more effectively, and experience less stress and anxiety. They're also more likely to be promoted at work and have stronger, more satisfying relationships. Yet despite its importance, true self-awareness remains surprisingly rare.

Studies suggest that while 95% of people believe they are self-aware, only 10-15% actually meet the criteria for self-awareness. This gap exists because self-awareness requires the courage to look honestly at ourselves, including our flaws and blind spots—something our ego naturally resists.

The Self-Awareness Spectrum

Self-awareness exists on a spectrum, from unconscious incompetence to conscious mastery:

- **Unconscious Incompetence:** You don't know what you don't know about yourself. Your emotional reactions seem to come from nowhere, and you often feel like a victim of circumstances.
- **Conscious Incompetence:** You begin to recognize patterns in your behavior and emotional responses, but you don't yet know how to change them.
- **Conscious Competence:** You can identify your emotional states and triggers as they occur, and you're developing skills to manage them effectively.

- **Unconscious Competence:** Emotional awareness and regulation have become second nature. You naturally respond rather than react to challenging situations.

The goal isn't perfection—it's progress along this spectrum. Each level brings greater freedom and more conscious choice in how you navigate life's challenges.

Recognizing Your Emotional Patterns

Identifying Emotional Triggers

Emotional triggers are specific situations, people, words, or memories that provoke strong emotional reactions. These reactions often seem disproportionate to the actual situation because they're connected to deeper patterns, past experiences, or core fears.

Common emotional triggers include:
- **Criticism or perceived judgment** from others
- **Feeling ignored or dismissed** in conversations or meetings
- **Unexpected changes** to plans or routines
- **Conflict or confrontation** with others
- **Feeling overwhelmed** by too many demands
- **Comparison** with others' achievements or lifestyles

The key to managing triggers isn't to eliminate them entirely—that's often impossible—but to recognize them quickly and choose your response consciously rather than reacting automatically.

Understanding Your Emotional Habits

Just as we develop physical habits, we also develop emotional habits—automatic patterns of feeling and responding that may have served us once but no longer align with our goals or values.

Examples of common emotional habits include:
- **Catastrophizing:** Automatically assuming the worst possible outcome
- **People-pleasing:** Prioritizing others' comfort over your own needs
- **Perfectionism:** Setting impossibly high standards and being overly critical of mistakes
- **Avoidance:** Withdrawing from challenging conversations or situations
- **Blame-shifting:** Focusing on others' faults rather than taking responsibility

These habits often develop as coping mechanisms during childhood or stressful periods in our lives. While they may have been protective at one time, they can become limiting patterns that prevent us from reaching our full potential.

The Role of Self-Talk
Your internal dialogue—the constant stream of thoughts running through your mind—profoundly shapes your emotional experience. This self-talk can be supportive and encouraging, or it can be harsh and self-defeating.

Self-aware individuals learn to notice the quality and content of their self-talk. They recognize when their inner voice becomes overly critical and develop the skill to reframe negative thoughts into more balanced, realistic perspectives.

For example, instead of thinking "I always mess up presentations," a self-aware person might reframe this as "I've had some challenging presentations in the past, and I can learn from those experiences to improve."

Physical Awareness
Emotions don't exist only in your mind—they manifest in your body through physical sensations. Developing awareness of these bodily signals can help you recognize emotions before they escalate into reactive behavior.

Common physical signs of emotional states include:
- Tension in shoulders or jaw when stressed or angry
- Butterflies in stomach when anxious or excited
- Tight chest when feeling overwhelmed or sad
- Clenched fists when frustrated or defensive
- Rapid heartbeat when nervous or passionate about something

By tuning into these physical cues, you can catch emotions early and choose how to respond rather than being swept away by them.

Tools for Building Self-Awareness

Mindful Self-Observation
Mindfulness—the practice of present-moment awareness without judgment—is one of the most powerful tools for developing self-awareness. It involves stepping back from your experience and observing your thoughts, emotions, and reactions as they occur.

Simple mindfulness practices for self-awareness include:

- Emotional check-ins: Several times throughout the day, pause and ask yourself, "What am I feeling right now? What thoughts are going through my mind?"
- Body scans: Take a few minutes to notice physical sensations from head to toe, identifying areas of tension or relaxation
- Breath awareness: Use your breath as an anchor to the present moment, noticing when your mind wanders and gently bringing attention back

The key is consistency rather than duration. Even 30 seconds of mindful observation can provide valuable insights into your emotional patterns.

Emotional Journaling

Writing about your emotional experiences creates distance between you and your emotions, allowing for greater objectivity and insight. Unlike a regular diary, emotional journaling focuses specifically on understanding your inner world.

Effective emotional journaling includes:
- Daily emotion tracking: Note your primary emotions throughout the day and what triggered them
- Pattern recognition: Look for recurring themes in your emotional responses
- Trigger analysis: When you have a strong reaction, write about what happened, what you felt, and what might have caused such an intense response
- Growth reflection: Regularly review past entries to notice progress and persistent challenges

Consider using prompts such as:
- "Today I felt most energized when..."
- "I noticed I got defensive when..."
- "The emotion that surprised me today was..."
- "I handled [challenging situation] better than usual by..."

Feedback Systems

While self-reflection is crucial, we all have blind spots—aspects of ourselves that we can't see clearly. Trusted friends, family members, or colleagues can provide valuable external perspectives on our emotional patterns and behaviors.

Creating effective feedback systems involves:
- **Choosing the right people**: Select individuals who know you well, care about your growth, and can provide honest but constructive feedback

- **Asking specific questions**: Instead of "How am I doing?" ask "What do you notice about how I handle stress?" or "When do you see me at my best?"
- **Creating safety**: Make it clear that you want honest feedback and won't become defensive or punish them for their honesty
- **Following up**: Check back with your feedback providers to see if they notice changes in your behavior over time

Remember, the goal isn't to change yourself to please others, but to gain insight into how your internal experience translates into external behavior.

Meditation and Reflection

Regular meditation practice creates space for deeper self-understanding by quieting the constant chatter of daily life. Even brief periods of meditation can help you:
- Observe thought patterns without getting caught up in them
- Notice emotional reactions without immediately acting on them
- Develop equanimity in the face of challenging emotions
- Cultivate self-compassion as you observe your human imperfections

If formal meditation feels intimidating, start with simple reflection practices:
- **Morning intention setting**: Spend five minutes considering how you want to show up emotionally during the day
- **Evening review**: Reflect on your emotional experiences and what you learned about yourself
- **Walking meditation**: Use a regular walk as an opportunity for mindful self-observation

Developing Emotional Vocabulary

Beyond "Fine" and "Okay"

Many people operate with a limited emotional vocabulary, using generic terms like "good," "bad," "fine," or "stressed" to describe complex inner experiences. This linguistic limitation restricts our ability to understand and communicate our emotional states effectively.

Expanding your emotional vocabulary allows for:
- Greater precision in identifying what you're actually feeling
- Better communication with others about your inner experience
- Increased emotional regulation through more accurate labeling
- Enhanced self-understanding through nuanced emotional awareness

Instead of "I feel bad," you might discover you feel:
- Disappointed about a specific outcome

- Frustrated with a particular situation
- Overwhelmed by too many demands
- Lonely despite being around people
- Anxious about an upcoming challenge

The Nuances of Feeling

Emotions exist on spectrums and often occur in combinations. Learning to distinguish between similar emotions helps you respond more appropriately to your inner experience.

For example, the anger family includes:
- **Irritation**: Mild annoyance at minor inconveniences
- **Frustration**: Feeling blocked from achieving a goal
- **Resentment**: Lingering anger about past treatment
- **Rage**: Intense, overwhelming anger
- **Indignation**: Anger at perceived injustice

Each of these requires different responses and coping strategies. Irritation might need a brief pause and reframing, while rage requires more intensive regulation techniques.

Cultural and Personal Influences

Your emotional vocabulary and expression are shaped by cultural background, family patterns, and personal experiences. Some cultures encourage emotional expression while others value emotional restraint. Some families discuss feelings openly while others avoid emotional topics entirely.

Understanding these influences helps you:
- Recognize inherited patterns that may not serve you
- Appreciate different emotional styles in relationships
- Choose conscious emotional expression rather than automatic cultural responses
- Develop emotional flexibility across different contexts

There's no "right" way to experience or express emotions, but awareness of your patterns allows for more intentional choices.

Reflection Questions

Take time to honestly consider these questions, perhaps writing your responses in a journal:
- **What emotions do you experience most frequently throughout your day?** Notice patterns in your emotional landscape. Are you often anxious, excited, frustrated,

content? What does this tell you about your current life circumstances and inner world?
- **What are your most consistent emotional triggers and patterns?** Identify the situations, people, or thoughts that reliably provoke strong emotional reactions. What themes do you notice? How do these patterns serve or limit you?
- **How accurately can you predict your emotional responses to different situations?** Self-awareness includes the ability to anticipate how you'll likely feel and react in various circumstances. Where are you most predictable? Where do you surprise yourself?

Action Steps

Begin a daily emotional awareness tracker using the provided template
Create a simple system for monitoring your emotional patterns. This might be as simple as noting your primary emotion and energy level three times per day, or as detailed as tracking specific triggers and responses. The key is consistency rather than perfection.

Practice the "emotional check-in" technique every few hours
Set reminders on your phone or computer to pause and ask yourself: "What am I feeling right now? What's happening in my body? What thoughts are going through my mind?" This practice builds the habit of emotional awareness throughout your day.

Identify three people who can provide honest feedback about your emotional patterns
Choose individuals who know you well in different contexts—perhaps a family member, a close friend, and a colleague. Ask them specific questions about your emotional patterns and be prepared to listen without defensiveness.

Self-awareness is not a destination but a lifelong journey of discovery. As you develop this foundational skill, you'll find that all other aspects of emotional intelligence become more accessible. You can't manage what you don't acknowledge, and you can't change what you don't understand. By committing to knowing yourself more deeply, you're taking the essential first step toward emotional mastery and authentic personal growth.

The journey of self-awareness requires patience, courage, and self-compassion. You'll discover things about yourself that you love and things you want to change. Both discoveries are valuable. Remember, the goal isn't to become perfect—it's to become conscious. With greater self-awareness comes greater choice, and with greater choice comes the power to create the life you truly want.

Chapter 3: Self-Regulation

Managing Your Emotions, Not Suppressing Them

Self-regulation is the second pillar of emotional intelligence and the key to turning self-awareness into positive action. While self-awareness helps you notice and understand your emotions, self-regulation empowers you to manage them—so you can respond thoughtfully rather than react impulsively. This chapter will show you how to move from emotional reactivity to emotional mastery, building resilience and composure in the process.

The Difference Between Control, Suppression, and Healthy Regulation

Emotional Control is often misunderstood. Many people believe it means suppressing or denying feelings, but true self-regulation is about understanding, accepting, and skillfully managing emotions—not bottling them up or letting them explode.

Suppression means pushing emotions out of awareness or pretending they don't exist. This can lead to increased stress, anxiety, and even physical health issues.

Control is sometimes associated with rigidity or forcefully holding emotions back, which can be exhausting and unsustainable.

Healthy Regulation is the ability to pause, process, and choose your response. It's about allowing emotions to inform you without letting them dictate your actions.

> ***Key insight:*** *Emotions are messengers, not masters. Healthy self-regulation means listening to those messages and responding in ways that serve your values and goals.*

Strategies for Emotional Self-Management: Pause, Reframe, Respond

1. Pause

The most powerful tool in self-regulation is the pause. When you notice a strong emotion, give yourself a moment before reacting. This creates space for conscious choice.

The Pause Principle: When you feel triggered, take a few deep breaths. Count to five, or excuse yourself from the situation if needed. This short break interrupts the automatic reaction cycle.

2. Reframe

Once you've paused, examine your thoughts. Are you interpreting the situation in the most helpful way?

- **Cognitive Reframing:** Challenge automatic negative thoughts. Is there another perspective? What else could be true? For example, instead of "They're ignoring me on purpose," consider "Maybe they're distracted or busy."
- **Ask yourself:** Is this thought true? Is it helpful? What would I say to a friend in this situation?

3. Respond

Choose a response that aligns with your values and goals, rather than reacting from habit or impulse.

- **Response vs. Reaction:** A reaction is automatic and driven by emotion; a response is intentional and guided by awareness.

Techniques: Breathing, Grounding, and Reframing Negative Thoughts

Breathing Techniques

- **Box Breathing:** Inhale for four counts, hold for four, exhale for four, hold for four. Repeat several times.
- **4-7-8 Breathing:** Inhale for four counts, hold for seven, exhale for eight. This calms the nervous system and reduces anxiety.

Grounding Exercises

- **5-4-3-2-1 Technique:** Notice five things you can see, four you can touch, three you can hear, two you can smell, one you can taste. This brings your attention to the present moment.
- **Physical Anchors:** Place your feet flat on the ground, press your hands together, or touch a textured object.

Reframing Negative Thoughts

- **Thought Record:** Write down the negative thought, the emotion it triggers, evidence for and against it, and a more balanced alternative.
- **Self-Compassion Statements:** " It's okay to feel this way. I can handle this. This feeling will pass."

How to Handle Anger, Anxiety, Disappointment, and Overwhelm

Anger
- Recognize early signs (tight jaw, clenched fists, heat).
- Use the pause and breathing techniques.
- Express anger assertively, not aggressively: "I feel frustrated when…" instead of blaming.

Anxiety
- Use grounding and slow breathing.
- Challenge catastrophic thinking: "What's the most likely outcome?"
- Focus on what you can control, and take small actions.

Disappointment
- Allow yourself to feel it—don't minimize or deny.
- Reframe: What can you learn? What's still within your power?
- Practice gratitude for what is going well.

Overwhelm
- Break tasks into small, manageable steps.
- Prioritize: What needs attention right now? What can wait?
- Ask for help or delegate where possible.

Building Emotional Resilience

Resilience is your ability to bounce back from setbacks and adapt to change. Self-regulation is at the heart of resilience.

- **Anticipate Triggers:** Know your stress points and plan how you'll respond.
- **Practice Regular Self-Care:** Sleep, nutrition, movement, and downtime all support emotional balance.
- **Reflect and Learn:** After a difficult episode, review what worked, what didn't, and what you'll try next time.
- **Use Time Wisely:** Schedule breaks and downtime to prevent emotional overload (see *Time That Matters* for more strategies).

Reflection: When Do You Struggle Most to Manage Your Emotions?

Are there certain situations, people, or times of day when self-regulation is hardest?
What physical or mental signs tell you you're about to lose control?
What beliefs or habits make it harder for you to pause and choose your response?

Action: Self-Regulation Practice Plan

- **Identify Your Triggers:** List the top three situations where you struggle to manage your emotions.
- **Choose Your Tools**: Select at least two techniques (breathing, grounding, reframing) to use in those situations.
- **Create a Pause Plan:** Decide what you'll do when you notice a strong emotion (e.g., count to ten, take a walk, write in a journal).
- **Track Your Progress:** Keep a daily log of situations where you practiced self-regulation. Note what worked and what you'd do differently next time.
- **Celebrate Small Wins:** Every time you choose a response over a reaction, acknowledge your progress.

Remember: Self-regulation is not about never feeling strong emotions. It's about learning to ride the wave without being swept away. Like any skill, it improves with practice, patience, and self-compassion. Mastering this pillar will empower you to handle life's challenges with greater calm, clarity, and confidence.

Chapter 4: Motivation

HARNESSING EMOTION FOR GROWTH. FUEL FOR ACHIEVEMENT

Motivation is the driving force behind every action you take. It's what gets you out of bed in the morning, keeps you working toward your goals, and sustains you through setbacks. In the context of emotional intelligence, motivation isn't just about willpower or external rewards—it's about understanding and channeling your emotions to fuel meaningful, lasting growth. This chapter explores how to tap into both intrinsic and extrinsic motivation, how your emotions can drive or derail your progress, and how to build the grit and optimism necessary to keep moving forward—even when the going gets tough.

The Role of Intrinsic vs. Extrinsic Motivation

- **Intrinsic Motivation** is the internal drive to pursue activities because they are inherently interesting or fulfilling. It's the satisfaction you get from mastering a skill, solving a problem, or contributing to something bigger than yourself. Intrinsic motivation is closely linked to your values, passions, and sense of purpose.
- **Extrinsic Motivation** comes from outside yourself—rewards like money, praise, grades, or avoiding punishment. While extrinsic motivators can be effective in the short term, research shows they rarely sustain effort or satisfaction over the long run.
- **Why does this matter?** When your motivation is primarily intrinsic, you're more likely to persist through challenges, experience greater well-being, and feel a deeper sense of accomplishment. When motivation is mostly extrinsic, your drive can fade as soon as the reward disappears or the pressure lifts[13].
- **Reflection:** Think about a time you achieved something meaningful. What motivated you—internal satisfaction or external rewards? How did that affect your experience and your results?

How Emotions Drive (or Derail) Your Goals and Habits

Emotions are powerful motivators. They can propel you toward your goals—or sabotage your efforts if left unchecked.

- **Positive emotions** like excitement, hope, and pride energize you to take action, persist through obstacles, and celebrate progress.
- **Negative emotions** like fear, frustration, or disappointment can either motivate you to change or cause you to give up, depending on how you manage them.

Emotional Triggers and Motivation:
When you feel inspired, you're more likely to start new projects or set ambitious goals. When you feel discouraged or anxious, you may procrastinate or abandon your efforts.

The Motivation-Emotion Cycle:
- **Emotion sparks motivation** (e.g., excitement about a new goal).
- **Action follows** (e.g., you start working toward the goal).
- **Progress creates more positive emotion** (e.g., satisfaction, pride).
- **Setbacks trigger negative emotions** (e.g., disappointment, frustration).

Your response to these emotions determines whether you persist or quit.

Key Insight: Emotionally intelligent people use their emotions as fuel, not as roadblocks. They recognize when negative feelings arise and have strategies to process and reframe them, so setbacks become learning opportunities rather than dead ends.

Building Grit, Optimism, and Perseverance

- Grit is the ability to persevere over the long haul, even when progress is slow or obstacles appear. It's a combination of passion and persistence.
- Optimism is the expectation that things will work out, even if you don't know exactly how. It's not blind positivity—it's realistic hopefulness that fuels perseverance.
- Perseverance is sticking with your goals, especially when motivation wanes.

How to Build Grit and Optimism:
- **Set clear, meaningful goals.** Goals that align with your values and sense of purpose are more motivating (see Goals That Matter).
- **Break big goals into small steps.** Celebrate each small win to maintain momentum.
- **Reframe setbacks.** Instead of seeing failure as a dead end, view it as feedback and a chance to improve.
- **Practice gratitude.** Focusing on what's going well—even in tough times—boosts optimism and resilience2.
- **Surround yourself with positive, motivated people.** Social support reinforces your own motivation and grit.
- **Practical Example:** When you encounter a setback, ask yourself: "What can I learn from this? How can I use this experience to get closer to my goal?"

Using Positive Emotions to Fuel Action and Bounce Back from Setbacks

Positive emotions are not just pleasant—they are powerful tools for motivation and resilience.

- Joy, enthusiasm, and pride increase your energy and creativity.
- Gratitude helps you focus on abundance rather than lack, making it easier to stay motivated.
- Hope keeps you looking forward, even when things are difficult.

How to Cultivate Positive Emotions:

- **Start a gratitude journal.** Write down three things you're grateful for each day2.
- **Celebrate progress, not just results.** Acknowledge every step forward, no matter how small.
- **Visualize success.** Imagine yourself achieving your goals and how that will feel.
- **Practice self-compassion.** Be kind to yourself when things don't go as planned—treat setbacks as part of the growth process.
- **Bouncing Back:** When you hit a roadblock, take a pause. Reflect on what's working, what you've already achieved, and what you can do differently next time. Use positive self-talk to encourage yourself forward3.

Reflection: What Motivates You? What Drains Your Drive?

Take a few moments to reflect on the following:

- What types of goals or activities give you the most energy and satisfaction?
- When you lose motivation, what emotions or situations are usually involved?
- How do you typically respond to setbacks? Do you bounce back quickly, or do you get stuck?
- What habits or people in your life boost your motivation? Which ones drain it?

Action: Motivation Map and Daily Practice

Create Your Motivation Map:

List your top three goals.

For each goal, write down:

- Why it matters to you (your intrinsic motivation)
- What emotions you feel when you think about this goal
- What obstacles or negative emotions might arise
- Strategies you'll use to stay motivated (gratitude, reframing, support, etc.)

Daily Practice:
- Each morning, review your motivation map and set an intention for the day.
- Use a journal to track your progress, emotions, and any setbacks.
- Celebrate small wins every day, and practice gratitude for your efforts and growth.

Remember: Motivation isn't something you either have or don't have—it's a skill you can build by understanding your emotions, aligning your goals with your values, and practicing resilience every day. When you harness your emotional intelligence for motivation, you unlock the energy and persistence needed to achieve what matters most to you.

Chapter 5: Empathy

UNDERSTANDING AND CONNECTING WITH OTHERS

Empathy is the bridge between self-awareness and meaningful relationships. It is the ability to sense, understand, and care about what others are feeling—without losing sight of your own perspective. In the context of emotional intelligence, empathy is not just a "nice-to-have" trait; it is essential for healthy relationships, effective leadership, and true collaboration. This chapter explores the nature of empathy, why it matters, and how you can develop practical empathy skills that transform your interactions and deepen your connections with others.

The Difference Between Empathy, Sympathy, and Compassion

Empathy is the ability to step into another person's emotional world—to feel with them, not just for them. It involves both recognizing and understanding another's feelings and, at times, sharing those feelings.

Sympathy is feeling pity or sorrow for someone else's misfortune but remaining at a distance from their emotional experience.

Compassion takes empathy a step further by adding a motivation to help or support the other person.

Empathy is about connection, not just observation. It is the foundation for trust, respect, and genuine human bonds.

Why Empathy Is Essential for Relationships, Leadership, and Collaboration

Empathy is the cornerstone of all meaningful relationships, whether personal or professional. Here's why it matters:
- **Relationships:** Empathy allows you to understand your partner's, friend's, or family member's emotional needs and perspectives. This understanding leads to deeper intimacy, fewer misunderstandings, and more effective conflict resolution.
- **Leadership:** Empathetic leaders inspire loyalty, foster engagement, and build psychologically safe environments where people can thrive. They are able to motivate and support their teams, especially during times of change or stress.

- **Collaboration:** Teams with high empathy communicate better, resolve conflicts more constructively, and are more innovative. Empathy enables you to see issues from multiple viewpoints, making it easier to find common ground and creative solutions.
- **Empathy** is also a key ingredient in social intelligence—the ability to navigate complex social situations and build strong networks.

Practical Empathy Skills

Empathy is a skill you can develop with intention and practice. Here are the core components:

1. Active Listening
- Give your full attention to the speaker. Put away distractions and make eye contact.
- Listen to understand, not just to reply. Notice tone, pace, and body language as well as words.
- Reflect back what you hear: "It sounds like you're feeling..."
- Validate emotions, even if you don't agree with the perspective: "That must be really tough for you."

2. Perspective-Taking
- Ask yourself, "What might this situation feel like from their point of view?"
- Be curious about their experiences, beliefs, and values.
- Avoid making assumptions or judgments. Instead, ask open-ended questions: "Can you tell me more about what that was like for you?"

3. Reading Nonverbal Cues
- Notice facial expressions, posture, gestures, and tone of voice.
- Pay attention to what is not being said—sometimes silence or withdrawal speaks volumes.
- If you sense a disconnect between words and body language, gently check in: "I hear you saying you're okay, but you seem upset. Is there more you'd like to share?"

4. Emotional Mirroring
- Subtly reflect the other person's emotions through your facial expressions and tone.
- Use supportive statements: "I can see why you'd feel that way."
- Be careful not to mimic or exaggerate—genuine mirroring builds trust, while insincerity erodes it.

Overcoming Empathy Fatigue and Setting Boundaries

Empathy is powerful, but it can also be draining—especially if you're highly sensitive or in a caregiving role. This is known as "empathy fatigue."

How to avoid empathy fatigue:
- **Recognize** your emotional limits. It's okay to step back and recharge.
- **Set boundaries:** You can care deeply without taking on responsibility for fixing everyone's problems.
- **Practice** self-care and seek support when needed.
- **Healthy boundaries** allow you to remain compassionate without becoming overwhelmed. Remember, you can be present for others while also protecting your own emotional well-being.

Reflection: When Do You Find It Easy—or Hard—to Empathize?

In what situations do you naturally feel empathy for others?

Are there certain people or circumstances where empathy is more difficult?

How do your own emotions or stress levels affect your ability to be empathetic?

What beliefs or habits might make it harder for you to connect with others' feelings?

Action: Empathy-Building Exercises
- **Active Listening Practice:** Choose one conversation each day to practice full, undistracted listening. Reflect back what you hear and validate the other person's feelings.
- **Perspective-Taking Journal:** After a challenging interaction, write about the situation from the other person's point of view. What might they have been feeling or needing?
- **Nonverbal Awareness:** For one day, focus on noticing nonverbal cues in your interactions. How do people's body language and tone add to or change the meaning of their words?
- **Empathy Check-In:** When you feel yourself becoming emotionally overwhelmed, pause and ask: "What's mine to carry, and what belongs to the other person?" Set a healthy boundary if needed.
- **Empathy Challenge:** Reach out to someone you don't usually connect with—at work, in your community, or even online. Ask about their experiences and listen with curiosity and openness.

Remember: Empathy is not about fixing or rescuing others, but about being present, understanding, and connecting. As you strengthen your empathy skills, you'll find your relationships become richer, your leadership more effective, and your sense of connection to others—and yourself—deepens.

Chapter 6: Social Skills

BUILDING STRONG, HEALTHY RELATIONSHIPS

Emotional Intelligence in Action

Social skills are the visible expression of emotional intelligence in action. They are the tools that allow us to connect, communicate, collaborate, and resolve conflict with others. Whether in our personal lives, workplaces, or communities, strong social skills are essential for building relationships that matter, fostering trust, and achieving shared goals. This chapter explores the core components of social skills, how emotional intelligence enhances them, and practical steps to strengthen your social effectiveness in every area of life.

Communication Mastery: Assertiveness, Feedback, and Conflict Resolution

Assertive Communication

Assertiveness is the ability to express your thoughts, feelings, and needs openly and respectfully, without infringing on the rights of others. It is the balance between passivity (not speaking up) and aggression (speaking up in a way that disrespects others).

- **Why it matters:** Assertive communication builds trust, sets healthy boundaries, and prevents resentment.
- **How to practice:** Use "I" statements ("I feel...", "I need..."), maintain steady eye contact, and speak clearly and calmly.
- **Example:** "I feel concerned when deadlines are missed because it affects the whole team. Can we discuss how to stay on track?"

Giving and Receiving Feedback

Feedback is essential for growth, both personally and in relationships. Emotionally intelligent feedback is specific, constructive, and delivered with empathy.

- **Giving feedback:** Focus on behaviors, not personalities. Be specific about what you observed, explain its impact, and suggest alternatives.
- **Receiving feedback:** Listen without interrupting, ask clarifying questions, and thank the person—even if the feedback is difficult to hear.

Conflict Resolution

Conflict is inevitable in any relationship, but with emotional intelligence, it becomes an opportunity for growth rather than division.

- **Approach conflict with curiosity, not blame.** Seek to understand the other person's perspective.
- **Use "win-win" thinking:** Aim for solutions that respect everyone's needs.
- **Manage your emotions:** Take breaks if needed, and return to the conversation when calm.
- **Apologize and forgive:** A sincere apology can repair trust; forgiveness frees you from holding onto resentment.

Navigating Social Dynamics: Influence, Teamwork, and Leadership

Influence Without Manipulation

Influence is about inspiring and motivating others, not controlling them. Emotionally intelligent influence is rooted in trust, authenticity, and mutual respect.

- Build rapport: Find common ground and show genuine interest in others.
- Model the behavior you want to see: People are more likely to follow your lead if your actions match your words.
- Encourage and empower: Help others see their strengths and potential.
- Teamwork: High-performing teams are built on trust, open communication, and respect for diversity.
- Emotional intelligence helps you: Recognize and appreciate different perspectives and strengths.
- Manage group emotions: Stay aware of the group's mood and address negativity or tension early.
- Share credit and celebrate wins together.

Leadership: Leaders with strong social skills inspire loyalty, foster collaboration, and create psychologically safe environments.
- Communicate vision and values clearly.
- Listen actively and seek input from all team members.
- Provide support and recognition.
- Handle setbacks and conflict with composure and fairness.

The Role of Emotional Intelligence in Digital Communication

Digital communication—emails, texts, social media—can easily lead to misunderstandings because it lacks tone, facial expressions, and body language. Emotional intelligence is crucial for maintaining connection and clarity online.

Pause before responding: Avoid reacting impulsively to digital messages.

Read between the lines: Notice what might be unsaid or misunderstood.

Use clear, positive language: Avoid sarcasm or ambiguous statements.

Set boundaries: Protect your time and energy by managing digital interruptions and expectations.

Repairing, Deepening, and Letting Go of Relationships with EQ

Repairing Relationships

Every relationship faces challenges. Emotional intelligence helps you:
- Acknowledge mistakes and take responsibility.
- Initiate honest conversations to clear misunderstandings.
- Seek to understand the other person's feelings and perspective.
- Work together to rebuild trust and set new agreements.

Deepening Relationships

- To deepen relationships, practice vulnerability and authenticity.
- Share your true thoughts and feelings.
- Ask meaningful questions and listen deeply.
- Show appreciation and gratitude regularly.
- Invest time and energy in shared experiences.

Letting Go with Grace

Sometimes, relationships run their course. Emotional intelligence enables you to:
- Recognize when a relationship is no longer healthy or supportive.
- Communicate your feelings honestly and kindly.
- Release resentment and wish the other person well.
- Reflect on what you learned and how you grew.

Reflection: Which Social Skills Do You Want to Strengthen?

Are there situations where you struggle to assert yourself?

How comfortable are you with giving and receiving feedback?

Do you find it easy or challenging to resolve conflicts constructively?

What is your greatest strength in teamwork or leadership? Where could you improve?

How do you handle digital communication and boundaries?

Are there relationships in your life that need repair, deepening, or closure?

Action: Social Skills Challenge

Choose one social skill (assertiveness, feedback, conflict resolution, teamwork, digital communication, or relationship repair) to focus on this week.

Set a specific goal (e.g., "I will assert myself at least once in a meeting," or "I will initiate a conversation to repair a strained relationship.")

Reflect daily on your experiences—what worked, what felt challenging, and what you learned.

Ask for feedback from someone you trust about your progress.

Celebrate your efforts and growth.

Remember: Social skills are not innate—they are learned and refined through practice and reflection. By applying emotional intelligence to your interactions, you will build relationships that matter, foster collaboration, and create a positive ripple effect in every area of your life.

Chapter 7: EQ in Action

EVERYDAY HABITS FOR EMOTIONAL INTELLIGENCE

Making Emotional Intelligence a Way of Life

Emotional intelligence (EQ) is not a one-time achievement but a daily practice—a set of habits and choices that shape how you think, feel, and interact with the world. This chapter is about making EQ a living, breathing part of your everyday life. By weaving self-awareness, self-regulation, motivation, empathy, and social skills into your routines at work, at home, and in your community, you create a foundation for resilience, fulfillment, and relationships that matter. Here's how to put emotional intelligence into action, one habit at a time.

Daily EQ Habits: Self-Check-ins, Gratitude, Emotional Labeling, and Mindful Pauses

1. Self-Check-ins

Begin and end your day by asking: "What am I feeling right now? Why?"

Use short, regular pauses throughout the day (e.g., before meetings, after a difficult conversation) to notice your emotional state.

This habit builds real-time self-awareness and prevents emotional buildup[1].

2. Gratitude Practice

Each morning or evening, write down three things you're grateful for.

Express appreciation to others—at work, at home, or in your community.

Gratitude shifts your focus from what's missing to what's working, fueling optimism and resilience[1].

3. Emotional Labeling

Get specific: Instead of "I feel bad," try "I feel disappointed," "anxious," or "overwhelmed."

Teach this habit to your children, team, or partner—emotional literacy is contagious.

Labeling emotions accurately helps you process and manage them more effectively[1].

4. Mindful Pauses

Schedule a few minutes each day to simply breathe and notice your thoughts and feelings without judgment.

Use mindful pauses during stressful moments to reset and choose your response.

Over time, this habit strengthens your ability to regulate emotions and respond thoughtfully[1].

How to Build EQ at Work, at Home, and in Your Community

At Work

Start meetings with a quick emotional check-in (e.g., "What's one word for how you're feeling today?").

Practice active listening—focus fully when colleagues speak, and reflect back what you hear.

Give and receive feedback with empathy, aiming for growth rather than criticism.

Use setbacks as learning opportunities, modeling resilience for your team[1].

At Home

Make emotional check-ins part of your family routine—ask kids or partners about their highs and lows each day.

Model healthy emotional expression and regulation.

Celebrate small wins and express gratitude for each other.

Use conflicts as chances to practice empathy and problem-solving together[1].

In Your Community

Volunteer or participate in group activities that foster connection and understanding.

Practice kindness and patience in everyday interactions—with neighbors, service workers, or strangers.

Support community initiatives that promote mental health and emotional well-being[1].

The Kaizen Approach: Small Steps for Big Emotional Growth

Kaizen, the Japanese philosophy of continuous improvement, teaches that small, consistent changes lead to big results over time. Apply Kaizen to your emotional intelligence:

Choose one EQ habit to focus on each week (e.g., daily gratitude, mindful pauses, or active listening).

Track your progress—use a journal or habit tracker to note successes and challenges.

Celebrate small wins and adjust your approach as needed.

Over time, these micro-habits compound, creating lasting transformation in your emotional life13.

Using Setbacks and Mistakes as EQ Growth Opportunities

No one practices emotional intelligence perfectly. Mistakes and setbacks are inevitable—and valuable.

When you react poorly or miss an EQ habit, pause and reflect: What triggered this? What could I do differently next time?

Reframe setbacks as learning moments rather than failures.

Share your growth process with others—modeling vulnerability and resilience encourages them to do the same13.

Remember: Progress, not perfection, is the goal.

Reflection: What's One EQ Habit You Can Start Today?

Which daily EQ habit feels most accessible or impactful for you right now?

Where in your routine could you insert a mindful pause or emotional check-in?

Who could benefit from you practicing more gratitude, empathy, or emotional labeling?

Write down your answers and commit to trying one new EQ habit for the next week.

Action: 30-Day EQ Habit Tracker

Your Challenge: For the next 30 days, choose one or more EQ habits (self-check-ins, gratitude, emotional labeling, mindful pauses, active listening, etc.) and track your daily practice.

Use a simple calendar, journal, or digital habit tracker.

At the end of each week, reflect: What's working? What's challenging? What positive changes do you notice?

At the end of 30 days, review your progress and celebrate your growth.

Sample Tracker:

Date	Habit Practiced?	Notes/Reflections
June 13	Yes	Felt calmer after morning pause
June 14	No	Forgot, will set reminder

Remember: Emotional intelligence is a journey built on daily choices. Every small habit you practice makes a difference—not just for you, but for everyone you interact with. By making EQ part of your everyday life, you create a ripple effect of understanding, resilience, and connection that extends far beyond yourself.

Chapter 8: EQ, Success, and the Things That Matter

The Ripple Effect of Emotional Intelligence

Emotional intelligence (EQ) is not just a personal asset—it is a force multiplier that amplifies every area of your life. In this chapter, we explore how EQ acts as the catalyst for meaningful change, goal achievement, effective time management, and the creation of relationships that truly matter. We'll also examine the ripple effect of EQ on families, teams, and communities, and why emotionally intelligent leadership is essential for inspiring, motivating, and supporting others. Finally, you'll reflect on where EQ has made the biggest difference in your life and create a plan to extend its impact even further.

How EQ Amplifies Change, Goal Achievement, Time Management, and Relationships

- **Change:** EQ is the foundation for navigating change with resilience and adaptability. When you are self-aware and able to regulate your emotions, you can approach change not as a threat but as an opportunity for growth. High EQ helps you manage the discomfort of uncertainty, reframe setbacks, and stay open to learning—core themes from *Change That Matters* and the Kaizen approach of continuous improvement.
- **Goal Achievement:** Motivation, optimism, and perseverance—core components of EQ—are what keep you moving toward your goals, even when progress is slow or obstacles arise. By understanding your emotional drivers and managing discouragement, you can sustain effort and celebrate small wins, transforming goals from distant dreams into daily realities (see *Goals That Matter* for practical strategies).
- **Time Management:** EQ empowers you to prioritize what truly matters, set healthy boundaries, and avoid the traps of procrastination or overwhelm. When you understand your emotional patterns, you can allocate your time and energy more effectively, focusing on high-impact activities that align with your values (see *Time That Matters* for more on this connection)13.
- **Relationships:** Perhaps nowhere is EQ more visible than in your relationships. Empathy, active listening, and social skills allow you to build trust, resolve conflicts, and nurture connections that support your growth. High EQ helps you recognize and repair relational ruptures, deepen intimacy, and foster collaboration—at home, at work, and in your community (see *Relationships That Matter* for a deeper dive)12.

The Ripple Effect: How Your EQ Impacts Teams, Families, and Communities

Your emotional intelligence is not confined to your own experience—it radiates outward, shaping the emotional climate of every group you're part of.

- **In families:** Your ability to manage stress, communicate openly, and show empathy creates a safe environment for others to express themselves and grow.
- **In teams:** EQ fosters psychological safety, trust, and collaboration. Teams with high collective EQ are more innovative, resilient, and productive2.
- **In communities:** Emotionally intelligent individuals contribute to healthier, more inclusive, and more supportive communities. They model compassion, resolve conflicts constructively, and inspire others to do the same.
- **The ripple effect is real:** Every time you choose to respond rather than react, to listen rather than judge, or to encourage rather than criticize, you set a positive example. Over time, these choices accumulate, creating a culture of emotional intelligence that benefits everyone around you12.

EQ and Leadership: Inspiring, Motivating, and Supporting Others

Emotionally intelligent leaders stand out—not just for what they achieve, but for how they inspire and elevate others.

- **Inspiration:** Leaders with high EQ articulate a compelling vision, connect it to shared values, and motivate others through encouragement and optimism.
- **Motivation:** They recognize and nurture the unique strengths of each team member, fostering engagement and a sense of purpose.
- **Support:** EQ leaders are attuned to the emotional climate, provide empathy and guidance during challenges, and create space for honest feedback and growth2.

Research and real-world experience show that EQ is the single most important differentiator of great leaders. It's not technical expertise or raw intelligence, but the ability to manage oneself and relate skillfully to others that inspires trust, loyalty, and high performance.

Reflection: Where Has EQ Made the Biggest Difference in Your Life?

Pause and consider:
- In what area—change, goals, time, or relationships—has your emotional intelligence had the most positive impact?

- How has EQ helped you overcome a specific challenge or achieve a meaningful success?
- Where do you notice the ripple effect of your emotional intelligence in your family, workplace, or community?
- What is one area where you'd like to amplify the impact of your EQ in the future?

Write down your reflections. These insights will help you recognize your growth and identify new opportunities to leverage EQ for even greater success.

Action: Your EQ "Ripple Effect" Plan

- **Identify your sphere of influence:** List the teams, relationships, or communities where your actions have an impact.
- **Choose one area to focus on:** Where could your EQ make the biggest difference right now? (e.g., supporting a team through change, deepening family relationships, mentoring a colleague)
- **Set a specific intention:** What will you do differently to model emotional intelligence? (e.g., practice active listening, offer encouragement, initiate honest conversations)
- **Track your impact:** Over the next month, note any changes in the emotional climate, trust, or collaboration in your chosen area.
- **Share your learning:** Discuss your experiences with others and invite them to join you in building a more emotionally intelligent culture.

Remember: Emotional intelligence is both a personal and a collective asset. As you strengthen your own EQ, you empower others to do the same—creating a ripple effect that transforms not just your life, but the lives of those around you. This is the heart of success that truly matters.

Chapter 9: Your 30-Day Emotional Intelligence Challenge

Emotional intelligence is not built in a day—it is cultivated through consistent, intentional practice. This chapter is your invitation to a 30-day challenge designed to help you systematically strengthen each pillar of EQ: self-awareness, self-regulation, motivation, empathy, and social skills. Through daily prompts, reflection, and practical exercises, you will track your progress, celebrate your wins, and lay the foundation for lifelong emotional growth. Whether you are new to EQ or looking to deepen your skills, this challenge will guide you, step by step, to a more emotionally intelligent and fulfilling life.

How to Build and Sustain EQ Growth

The 30-day challenge is structured to build your emotional intelligence one day at a time. Each week focuses on a specific pillar, layering skills so that by the end of the month, you will have practiced and integrated all five core competencies.

Week 1: Self-Awareness
1. Daily prompts to help you notice and name your emotions.
2. Journaling exercises to identify patterns, triggers, and emotional habits.
3. Mindfulness practices to increase present-moment awareness.

Week 2: Self-Regulation
1. Techniques to pause, reframe, and respond rather than react.
2. Breathing, grounding, and thought-challenging exercises.
3. Strategies for managing anger, anxiety, disappointment, and overwhelm.

Week 3: Motivation
1. Reflection on intrinsic vs. extrinsic motivation.
2. Daily gratitude and optimism boosters.
3. Exercises to set meaningful goals, map your motivation, and build perseverance.

Week 4: Empathy and Social Skills
1. Active listening and perspective-taking practices.
2. Empathy-building conversations and nonverbal awareness.
3. Social skills challenges: assertiveness, feedback, conflict resolution, and digital communication.
4. Each day, you'll complete a short exercise or reflection. At the end of each week, you'll review your progress and set intentions for the next stage.

Daily Prompts and Practices

Here is a sample structure for your 30-day journey:

Day 1-7: Self-Awareness
1. Morning check-in: "What am I feeling right now? Why?"
2. Track emotional highs and lows in a journal.
3. Identify your top three emotional triggers.
4. Practice mindful breathing for two minutes.
5. Reflect: "What did I learn about myself today?"

Day 8-14: Self-Regulation
1. Notice when you feel triggered—pause and breathe before responding.
2. Reframe a negative thought each day.
3. Use grounding techniques during stressful moments.
4. Practice the 24-hour rule: delay important decisions when emotions run high.
5. Reflect: "When did I choose a response over a reaction?"

Day 15-21: Motivation
1. Write down one thing you're grateful for each morning.
2. Set a daily intention aligned with your values.
3. Celebrate a small win each day.
4. Visualize success and how it will feel.
5. Reflect: "What kept me motivated today? What drained me?"

Day 22-30: Empathy and Social Skills
1. Practice active listening in one conversation per day.
2. Ask someone about their day and listen without interrupting.
3. Notice and respond to nonverbal cues.
4. Give or receive feedback with empathy.
5. Initiate a meaningful conversation or repair a strained relationship.
6. Reflect: "How did empathy or social skill change my interactions today?"

Tracking Progress and Celebrating Wins

Use a 30-Day EQ Tracker:

Create a simple table or use a journal to record your daily practice, insights, and any challenges. At the end of each week, review your notes and acknowledge your growth.

Day	Focus Area	Practice Completed?	Insights/Reflections
1	Self-Awareness	Yes	Noticed I get tense at work
2	Self-Awareness	Yes	Felt calmer after journaling

Celebrate Milestones:

At the end of each week and at the end of the challenge, reward yourself for your commitment—whether with a treat, a walk in nature, or sharing your progress with a friend.

Reflection: What Changed After 30 Days?

At the end of your challenge, take time to reflect:

- What new habits or insights have you gained?
- How have your emotions, relationships, or sense of purpose shifted?
- Which EQ skills feel most natural, and which need more practice?
- Where did you struggle, and what did you learn from those moments?
- How will you continue your EQ journey beyond this challenge?

Write your reflections in your journal or share them with a trusted friend or group.

Action: Share Your EQ Journey with Others

Growth is magnified when shared. Consider:

- Telling a friend, family member, or colleague about your 30-day challenge.
- Starting a small group or online community to practice EQ together.
- Offering encouragement and support to others who want to build their emotional intelligence.

Your journey can inspire others and create a ripple effect of emotional intelligence in your circles and beyond.

Remember: Emotional intelligence is a lifelong practice. The skills and habits you develop over these 30 days are just the beginning. Continue to reflect, practice, and connect—your future self (and those around you) will thank you.

Appendices & Resources

The appendices and resources section is designed to make *Emotional Intelligence That Matters* a practical, actionable guide—providing you with the tools, templates, and support needed to continue your EQ growth long after you finish the book. Use these materials to deepen your self-understanding, track your progress, and connect with others on the same journey.

1. EQ Self-Assessment Worksheet

Evaluate your strengths and growth areas across the five pillars of emotional intelligence:

- Self-awareness
- Self-regulation
- Motivation
- Empathy
- Social skills

Instructions:

- Rate yourself on a scale of 1 (rarely) to 5 (consistently) for each statement.
- Reflect on your lowest and highest scores.
- Identify 1-2 areas for focused improvement.

Sample Statements:

- I can accurately name my emotions as I experience them.
- I pause and think before reacting in emotionally charged situations.
- I persist in my goals even when motivation drops.
- I listen deeply and validate others 'feelings.
- I handle conflict with calm and respect.

2. Emotional Self-Awareness Journal Template

A daily or weekly journal to deepen your understanding of emotional patterns.

Template:
- Date:
- Situation/Event:
- Emotions Felt (be specific):
- Physical sensations:

- Trigger(s):
- My response:
- What helped/hindered my regulation?
- What I learned:
- What I'll try next time:

3. Self-Talk Reframing & Regulation Scripts

Practice shifting unhelpful inner dialogue to more supportive, realistic self-talk.

Examples:

Old: "I always mess this up."
New: "I've struggled before, but I can improve with practice."

Old: "I can't handle this."
New: "This is tough, but I have handled challenges before."

Instructions:
- Identify a recurring negative thought.
- Write a balanced, encouraging alternative.
- Practice using your new script in real situations.

4. Empathy & Communication Practice Guides

Active Listening Checklist:
- Maintain eye contact (if appropriate).
- Listen without interrupting.
- Reflect back what you heard ("So you're feeling…").
- Validate the other's experience ("That sounds difficult.").

Empathy-Building Exercise:
- Each day, ask someone a meaningful question and listen fully.
- Practice perspective-taking: "What might this feel like from their point of view?"

Feedback Framework:
- Focus on behavior, not personality.
- Be specific and constructive.
- Offer suggestions or support.
- Receive feedback with openness and gratitude.

5. 30-Day EQ Challenge Tracker

A printable or digital table to help you build daily EQ habits.

Day	Focus Area	Practice Completed?	Notes/Reflections
1	Self-Awareness	Yes/No	
2	Self-Regulation	Yes/No	
3	Social Skills	Yes/No	

Use this tracker to monitor your daily EQ practice, jot down insights, and celebrate progress.

6. Recommended Books, Podcasts, and Apps

Books:
- Emotional Intelligence by Daniel Goleman
- *The EQ Edge* by Steven J. Stein & Howard E. Book
- *Dare to Lead* by Brené Brown
- *Crucial Conversations* by Patterson, Grenny, McMillan & Switzler

Podcasts:
- The Science of Happiness
- The Emotional Intelligence Podcast
- Unlocking Us with Brené Brown

Apps:
- Moodnotes (emotional tracking & reframing)
- Headspace or Calm (mindfulness & self-regulation)
- Daylio (mood journaling)

7. Further Reading & Support Communities

- Six Seconds (emotional intelligence resources and assessments)
- Greater Good Science Center (UC Berkeley)
- Mindful.org (mindfulness practices)

- Online EQ forums and discussion groups (e.g., LinkedIn, Reddit)

8. Final Reflection & Series Roadmap

Key Questions for Ongoing EQ Growth:
- What new EQ habits do I want to sustain?
- Who can support me as I continue this journey?
- How will I measure my progress and celebrate growth?
- How does my EQ amplify my goals, time, and relationships?

How Emotional Intelligence Amplifies the Series:
EQ is the foundation for change, goal achievement, time management, and relationships.

- Use your EQ skills to revisit and deepen your progress in other *About Things That Matter* books.

Invitation to the Community:
- Share your journey with the About Things That Matter community.
- Connect with others for encouragement, accountability, and shared learning.

Preview of Future Books:
- *Health That Matters*: Foundations for physical aPhysicall well-being.
- *Money That Matters*: Financial intelligence aligned with your values.
- *Purpose That Matters*: Discovering and living your unique contribution.

These resources are yours to revisit and share. Use them to keep emotional intelligence alive in your daily life—and to help others do the same. Emotional intelligence is a lifelong journey, and every tool, reflection, and connection strengthens your ability to create a life that truly matters.

Bibliography

Major Research Foundations Referenced
- Harvard's Grant Study – 80-year longitudinal study on human flourishing.
- Stanford University research – Growth mindset and achievement, notably work by Dr. Carol Dweck.
- MIT – Studies on habit formation and behavioral change.
- Organizational psychology research – high-performance teamwork and support.

Explicitly Cited or Recommended Books
- The Art of Gathering by Priya Parker
- Dare to Lead by Brené Brown
- Never Eat Alone by Keith Ferrazzi
- Radical Candor by Kim Scott
- As a Man Thinketh by James Allen (cited for foundational life philosophy)

Recommended Podcasts
- We Can Do Hard Things with Glennon Doyle
- The Science of Happiness (Greater Good Science Center)
- Unlocking Us with Brené Brown

Digital Tools and Online Communities
- Meetup.com – Find local and interest-based groups and events.
- Lunchclub – Build professional connections.
- Reddit – r/relationships and r/DecidingToBeBetter.

Apps for Intentional Connection
- WhatsApp, Signal – Secure, private messaging and groups.
- Marco Polo – Personal, asynchronous video chat.
- Zoom, Google Meet – Virtual meetups and group calls.
- Slack, Discord – Community and project-based communication.
- Gratitude app – Journaling and daily gratitude prompts.

Research Literature & Classic Works
- Grant, G., et al. (Harvard's Grant Study)
- Dweck, C. S. – Mindset research
- Goleman, D. – Emotional intelligence and social psychology

Series Cross-References

Books from the *About Things That Matter* series provide foundational pillars and are referenced throughout for integrated personal growth:

- Change That Matters – JC Ryan
- Goals That Matter – JC Ryan
- Time That Matters – JC Ryan
- The Connection Code – JC Ryan

Notable Quotes/Influences
- Jim Rohn on the influence of your closest relationships ("You are the average of the five people you spend the most time with").
- Brené Brown on vulnerability and connection.

PART 2 – HAPPINESS THAT MATTERS

To everyone who has ever searched for happiness in all the wrong places, only to discover it was within their reach all along. May you find the courage to define joy on your own terms and the wisdom to nurture it daily.

"Happiness is not a destination, it is a way of life. It's not something you postpone for the future; it is something you design for the present." — ***Jim Rohn***

Happiness That Matters
The Habits and Mindset of Lasting Fulfillment

About Things That Matter
A Self-Improvement Series for Success

Book 6

JC Ryan

About This Book

WHY HAPPINESS IS THE FOUNDATION FOR A LIFE THAT MATTERS

Happiness is not a luxury; it's a necessity for a life well-lived. Yet in our achievement-oriented culture, we often treat happiness as the reward we'll claim after we've accomplished everything else. We tell ourselves we'll be happy when we get the promotion, lose the weight, find the relationship, or reach the financial milestone. This approach fundamentally misunderstands the relationship between happiness and success.

The truth is that happiness is not the result of success; it's often the precursor to it. Happy people are more creative, more resilient, more collaborative, and more likely to achieve their goals. They build stronger relationships, make better decisions, and contribute more meaningfully to their communities. Happiness doesn't just feel good—it does good.

This book challenges you to rethink everything you thought you knew about happiness. It's not about positive thinking or pretending problems don't exist. It's about developing the habits, mindset, and practices that create genuine fulfillment—the kind that sustains you through both triumph and adversity.

As part of the "About Things That Matter" series, this book builds on the foundation laid in our previous volumes. You've learned to set purpose-driven goals, manage your time effectively, and navigate change with confidence. Now we explore how happiness amplifies all of these efforts, creating a life that is not just successful by external measures, but deeply satisfying by your own standards.

This book is designed to be both philosophical and practical. You'll explore the science behind happiness while learning specific techniques to increase your well-being. You'll examine common myths about what makes people happy while discovering what actually works. Most importantly, you'll develop a personalized approach to happiness that aligns with your values, goals, and circumstances.

Each chapter includes reflection questions to deepen your self-awareness and action steps to implement what you've learned. The 30-day challenge in Chapter 8 provides a structured way to build lasting happiness habits using the Kaizen principle of small, continuous improvements.

This book integrates seamlessly with the other volumes in the "About Things That Matter" series. Your happiness journey will be enhanced by effective goal-setting, time management, and relationship skills. Conversely, your success in those areas will be amplified by the foundation of genuine well-being this book helps you build.

Chapter 1 – Rethinking Happiness

BEYOND THE MYTHS

Most of what we've been taught about happiness is wrong. We've been conditioned to believe that happiness comes from external sources—wealth, achievements, possessions, or other people's approval. We've been told that happy people are simply lucky, that some are born with a "happiness gene" while others are doomed to struggle. These myths not only limit our potential for joy but actively work against our well-being.

The Happiness Myths That Hold Us Back

Myth 1: Happiness Equals Wealth and Possessions

Perhaps no myth is more pervasive than the belief that money buys happiness. While financial security is important for meeting basic needs, research consistently shows that beyond a certain point—roughly $75,000 annually in most developed countries—additional income does not significantly increase happiness.

Studies indicate that higher income is associated with less daily sadness but not necessarily more daily happiness. Money can reduce distress but is not a reliable source of sustained joy. In fact, the pursuit of wealth as an end in itself often leads to what researchers call the "hedonic treadmill"—a cycle where people adapt to new levels of comfort and constantly need more to feel satisfied.

The problem isn't money itself, but making it the primary measure of success and happiness. When we tie our self-worth to our net worth, we set ourselves up for disappointment and anxiety.

Myth 2: Happiness Is the Absence of Negative Emotions

Many people believe that to be truly happy, they must eliminate sadness, anger, frustration, and disappointment from their lives. This myth is not only unrealistic but counterproductive. Happiness is not the absence of negative emotions—it's the ability to experience the full range of human feelings without being overwhelmed by them.

Research shows that people who try to suppress negative emotions often experience more distress, not less. Authentic happiness includes resilience—the capacity to feel difficult emotions, learn from them, and bounce back stronger. The goal isn't to eliminate sadness but to develop the skills to navigate it effectively.

Myth 3: Happiness Is a Destination
Our culture promotes "destination addiction"—the belief that happiness is something to be achieved rather than experienced. We tell ourselves we'll be happy when we get the promotion, lose the weight, find the perfect partner, or retire. This mindset keeps happiness perpetually out of reach.

In reality, happiness is more about the journey than the destination. It's a state of mind and a way of being that can be cultivated through daily habits, attitudes, and choices. When we stop waiting for happiness and start creating it, everything changes.

Myth 4: Happy People Are Just Lucky
Some people seem naturally happier than others, leading to the belief that happiness is largely determined by genetics or circumstances beyond our control. While research suggests that about 50% of happiness is influenced by our genetic "set point," this leaves substantial room for intentional cultivation.

Studies show that only about 10% of happiness is determined by external circumstances—income, marital status, job, health, and other life conditions. The remaining 40% is within our control, influenced by our thoughts, behaviors, and daily practices. This means we have significant power to increase our well-being through intentional action.

The True Nature of Happiness

Happiness as Fulfillment, Not Just Pleasure
True happiness is better understood as fulfillment rather than pleasure. While pleasurable experiences contribute to well-being, lasting happiness comes from meaning, purpose, and alignment with our values. It's the difference between hedonic well-being (feeling good) and eudaimonic well-being (living well).

Hedonic happiness is temporary and often dependent on external circumstances. Eudaimonic happiness is more stable and comes from within. It's the satisfaction of knowing you're living according to your principles, contributing to something larger than yourself, and growing as a person.

The Role of Meaning and Purpose
Research consistently shows that people who have a strong sense of purpose report higher levels of happiness and life satisfaction. Purpose provides direction, motivation, and resilience during difficult times. It connects our daily actions to something meaningful and helps us weather the inevitable storms of life.

Your purpose doesn't have to be grandiose or world-changing. It might be raising your children with love and wisdom, excelling in your profession, contributing to your community, or pursuing personal growth. What matters is that it resonates with your values and gives your life direction.

The Happiness Set Point: What You Can and Can't Control
Understanding the happiness set point is crucial for realistic expectations and effective action. While you can't control your genetic predisposition or change your past, you have significant influence over your present and future well-being.

The factors within your control include:
- Your daily habits and routines
- How you interpret and respond to events
- The relationships you cultivate
- The goals you pursue
- The meaning you create from your experiences
- Your physical health and self-care practices

Success and Happiness: Which Comes First?

Conventional wisdom suggests that success leads to happiness—work hard, achieve your goals, and happiness will follow. Research reveals the opposite is often true: happiness tends to precede success, not follow it.

Happy people are:
- More creative and innovative
- Better at problem-solving
- More resilient in the face of setbacks
- More likely to take positive risks
- Better at building relationships
- More productive and engaged at work

This doesn't mean you should abandon your goals or stop striving for achievement. Rather, it suggests that cultivating happiness as you pursue your goals will make you more likely to achieve them and more satisfied when you do.

The Science of Sustainable Happiness

Modern positive psychology has identified several key components of lasting happiness, often summarized in the PERMA model:

P - Positive Emotions: Joy, gratitude, serenity, interest, hope, pride, amusement, inspiration, awe, and love

E - Engagement: The experience of flow, where you're fully absorbed in activities that challenge your skills

R - Relationships: Social connections and the feeling of being loved and supported

M - Meaning: Serving something larger than yourself and feeling that your life has purpose

A - Accomplishment: The satisfaction of achieving goals and mastering skills

Each element contributes to well-being independently, and together they create a robust foundation for lasting happiness.

Reflection: What Does Happiness Mean to You?

Before moving forward, take time to examine your own beliefs and experiences with happiness:

1. **Personal Definition**: How do you currently define happiness? Has this definition changed over time?
2. **Happiness Myths**: Which of the common myths about happiness have influenced your thinking? How might these beliefs be limiting your well-being?
3. **Peak Experiences**: Think of times when you felt genuinely happy and fulfilled. What were the circumstances? What elements were present?
4. **Values Alignment**: When do you feel most satisfied with your life? How do these moments relate to your core values?
5. **Current State**: On a scale of 1-10, how would you rate your current level of happiness? What factors contribute to this rating?

Action: Your Personal Happiness Inventory

Complete this comprehensive assessment to understand your current happiness landscape:

Life Satisfaction Assessment
Rate each area of your life from 1 (very dissatisfied) to 10 (very satisfied):

- Career and work
- Relationships and social connections
- Physical health and energy
- Financial security
- Personal growth and learning
- Recreation and fun
- Contribution and service
- Spiritual or philosophical well-being

Happiness Habits Audit
Evaluate how often you engage in research-backed happiness practices:

- Expressing gratitude (daily, weekly, rarely, never)
- Engaging in physical exercise
- Spending quality time with loved ones
- Pursuing meaningful goals
- Practicing mindfulness or meditation
- Helping others or volunteering
- Engaging in activities that create "flow"
- Getting adequate sleep and rest

Happiness Obstacles Identification
Identify what currently interferes with your happiness:

- Negative thought patterns
- Toxic relationships
- Overwhelming stress or busyness
- Lack of purpose or direction
- Poor physical health habits
- Financial worries
- Comparison with others
- Perfectionism or unrealistic expectations

Values and Purpose Clarity
Reflect on your core values and sense of purpose:

- What matters most to you in life?
- What activities make you feel most alive and engaged?

- How do you want to be remembered?
- What contribution do you want to make to the world?
- When do you feel most authentic and true to yourself?

This inventory will serve as your baseline as you work through the remaining chapters. Return to it periodically to track your progress and adjust your approach as needed.

Chapter Summary

Rethinking happiness means moving beyond cultural myths that equate it with wealth, pleasure, or external achievements. True happiness is more nuanced and deeply personal, rooted in meaning, purpose, and authentic self-expression. While genetics and circumstances play a role, you have significant control over your well-being through your daily choices, habits, and mindset. Understanding the science of happiness—including the PERMA model and the relationship between success and well-being—provides a foundation for building lasting fulfillment. The journey begins with honest self-assessment and a commitment to defining happiness on your own terms.

Chapter 2 – The Foundations of Lasting Happiness

Building lasting happiness is like constructing a house—you need a solid foundation before you can add the walls, roof, and finishing touches. This chapter explores the core elements that support sustainable well-being, giving you the framework to build a genuinely fulfilling life.

The PERMA Model: Your Happiness Blueprint

Developed by psychologist Martin Seligman, the PERMA model identifies five essential elements of well-being. Unlike temporary pleasures that fade quickly, these elements create lasting satisfaction and resilience.

Positive Emotions: The Fuel of Well-Being

Positive emotions do more than make us feel good—they broaden our thinking, build our resources, and create upward spirals of well-being. When we experience joy, gratitude, love, or hope, our minds become more creative, our relationships stronger, and our resilience deeper.

The key is to cultivate positive emotions intentionally rather than waiting for them to occur naturally. This might involve:

- Savoring pleasant experiences by paying full attention to them
- Practicing gratitude for both big and small blessings
- Engaging in activities that bring you joy
- Sharing good news with others to amplify positive feelings
- Creating positive anticipation by planning enjoyable activities

Engagement: Finding Your Flow

Engagement refers to the experience of flow—those moments when you're completely absorbed in an activity, time seems to disappear, and you feel fully alive. Flow occurs when your skills are well-matched to the challenge at hand, creating a state of effortless concentration.

To increase engagement in your life:

- Identify activities that naturally create flow for you
- Seek challenges that stretch your abilities without overwhelming you
- Minimize distractions during important activities
- Develop your strengths and talents
- Look for opportunities to use your skills in new ways

Relationships: The Heart of Happiness

Perhaps no factor is more important for happiness than the quality of our relationships. Studies consistently show that people with strong social connections are happier, healthier, and live longer than those who are isolated.

The Harvard Study of Adult Development, which has followed participants for over 80 years, found that good relationships keep us happier and healthier. It's not the number of relationships that matters, but their quality. One close, supportive relationship can be more valuable than dozens of superficial connections.

Building strong relationships requires:
- Investing time and attention in the people who matter most
- Practicing empathy and active listening
- Being vulnerable and authentic in your connections
- Offering support during difficult times
- Celebrating others' successes genuinely
- Resolving conflicts constructively

Meaning: Your North Star

Meaning comes from serving something larger than yourself and feeling that your life has purpose. This might involve your family, career, faith, community service, or personal mission. Meaning provides direction during uncertainty and strength during adversity.

Research shows that people who have a strong sense of purpose:
- Live longer and have better physical health
- Are more resilient during difficult times
- Experience greater life satisfaction
- Are more motivated and engaged in their activities
- Have stronger immune systems

To cultivate meaning:
- Identify your core values and live according to them
- Connect your daily activities to larger purposes
- Contribute to causes you care about
- Reflect on how your work and relationships serve others
- Create a personal mission statement
- Engage in activities that align with your beliefs

Accomplishment: The Satisfaction of Achievement

Accomplishment involves pursuing goals and mastering skills for their own sake, not just for the external rewards they bring. This element of well-being comes from the satisfaction of growth, progress, and achievement.

Healthy accomplishment is characterized by:
- Setting goals that align with your values
- Focusing on personal growth rather than comparison with others
- Celebrating progress, not just final outcomes
- Learning from setbacks and failures
- Pursuing mastery in areas that matter to you
- Balancing achievement with other aspects of well-being

The Role of Purpose, Meaning, and Values

Your values are your internal compass, guiding your decisions and actions toward what matters most to you. When your life aligns with your values, you experience greater satisfaction and authenticity. When there's a disconnect, you feel stressed, conflicted, and unfulfilled.

Identifying Your Core Values

Values are fundamental beliefs about what's important in life. They're different from goals—while goals are specific outcomes you want to achieve, values are ongoing principles that guide how you want to live. Common core values include:
- Family and relationships
- Health and well-being
- Personal growth and learning
- Creativity and self-expression
- Service and contribution
- Adventure and exploration
- Security and stability
- Achievement and success
- Spirituality and meaning
- Freedom and autonomy

Living Your Values Daily

Once you've identified your core values, the challenge is living them consistently. This requires:
- Making decisions that align with your values, even when it's difficult

- Regularly evaluating whether your activities support your values
- Adjusting your commitments to better reflect your priorities
- Communicating your values to others
- Creating systems and habits that support value-based living

The Happiness Set Point: What You Can and Can't Control

Understanding what influences happiness helps you focus your energy where it can make the greatest difference. Research suggests that happiness is influenced by three main factors:

Genetic Set Point (50%)

Your genetic inheritance influences your baseline level of happiness. Some people are naturally more optimistic, resilient, or emotionally stable than others. While you can't change your genes, you can work with your natural tendencies rather than against them.

Life Circumstances (10%)

External factors like income, marital status, job, and health have less impact on happiness than most people assume. This doesn't mean these factors don't matter, but that their influence is smaller than we typically believe.

Intentional Activities (40%)

This is where you have the most control. Your thoughts, behaviors, and daily practices significantly influence your well-being. This includes:

- How you interpret events
- The habits you cultivate
- The relationships you build
- The goals you pursue
- The meaning you create
- The gratitude you practice

The Impact of Gratitude, Optimism, and Self-Acceptance

Three mindset elements have particularly strong effects on happiness: gratitude, optimism, and self-acceptance.

Gratitude: The Gateway to Abundance

Gratitude is one of the most powerful happiness practices. It shifts your focus from what's lacking to what's present, from problems to blessings. Grateful people are more optimistic, have stronger relationships, sleep better, and have stronger immune systems.

Effective gratitude practices include:
- Keeping a daily gratitude journal
- Writing thank-you notes to people who've helped you
- Expressing appreciation regularly to family and friends
- Practicing gratitude meditation
- Looking for silver linings in difficult situations
- Appreciating simple pleasures and everyday moments

Optimism: The Power of Positive Expectations

Optimism isn't about denying problems or pretending everything is perfect. It's about maintaining hope and looking for opportunities even in difficult circumstances. Optimistic people are more resilient, have better physical health, and achieve their goals more often.

You can cultivate optimism by:
- Challenging negative predictions about the future
- Looking for evidence that contradicts pessimistic thoughts
- Focusing on what you can control rather than what you can't
- Practicing solution-focused thinking
- Surrounding yourself with positive, supportive people
- Celebrating small wins and progress

Self-Acceptance: The Foundation of Inner Peace

Self-acceptance means acknowledging your strengths and weaknesses without harsh self-judgment. It's about treating yourself with the same kindness you'd show a good friend. Self-accepting people are more resilient, have better relationships, and experience less anxiety and depression.

Self-acceptance practices include:
- Practicing self-compassion during difficult times
- Challenging your inner critic
- Focusing on growth rather than perfection
- Acknowledging your accomplishments and progress
- Forgiving yourself for past mistakes
- Embracing your authentic self rather than trying to be someone else

Reflection: When Have You Felt Truly Happy?

Take time to explore your personal experiences with genuine happiness:

1. **Peak Happiness Moments**: Describe three times in your life when you felt genuinely happy and fulfilled. What were the circumstances? What elements were present?
2. **PERMA Analysis**: Looking at your peak happiness moments, which elements of PERMA were most prominent? How can you incorporate more of these elements into your current life?
3. **Values Alignment**: During your happiest times, how well was your life aligned with your core values? What does this tell you about the relationship between values and happiness?
4. **Meaning and Purpose**: When have you felt most connected to something larger than yourself? How did this sense of meaning contribute to your well-being?
5. **Relationship Quality**: How did the quality of your relationships during happy periods compare to other times? What role did social connection play in your happiness?

Action: Define Your "Why" for Happiness

Creating a compelling reason for pursuing happiness will motivate you through the challenges ahead:

Step 1: Clarify Your Motivation

Write detailed answers to these questions:

- Why is happiness important to you personally?
- How would greater happiness improve your life?
- What would you be able to give others if you were happier?
- How might happiness help you achieve your other goals?
- What's the cost of continuing with your current level of happiness?

Step 2: Envision Your Happy Life

Create a vivid picture of what your life would look like if you were truly happy:

- How would you feel each day?
- How would you interact with others?
- What activities would fill your time?
- How would you handle stress and challenges?
- What would others notice about you?

Step 3: Identify Your Values-Based Why

Connect your desire for happiness to your deepest values:
- Which of your core values would be better served by greater happiness?
- How does happiness align with your life purpose?
- What contribution could you make if you were happier?

Step 4: Create Your Happiness Mission Statement

Write a brief statement that captures why happiness matters to you:

"I am committed to cultivating happiness because..."

Step 5: Establish Your Commitment

Make a formal commitment to your happiness journey:
- What are you willing to do to increase your well-being?
- What habits are you willing to change?
- What support will you seek?
- How will you measure progress?

This foundation will support everything else you build in your happiness journey. Remember, lasting happiness isn't about constant joy—it's about creating a life of meaning, connection, and authentic fulfillment that can weather any storm.

Chapter 3 – Habits That Build Happiness

Happiness isn't just a feeling—it's a practice. Like physical fitness, well-being improves through consistent, intentional habits that compound over time. This chapter explores the daily practices that research shows can significantly increase your happiness and life satisfaction.

The Science of Happiness Habits

Habits are the building blocks of our daily experience. Research suggests that about 40% of our daily actions are habits rather than conscious decisions. This means that by changing your habits, you can literally rewire your brain for greater happiness.

The key is understanding that happiness habits work through neuroplasticity—your brain's ability to form new neural pathways. Each time you practice gratitude, perform an act of kindness, or engage in mindfulness, you strengthen the neural networks associated with well-being.

Daily Practices: The Core Four

Four practices have the strongest scientific support for increasing happiness: gratitude, savoring, mindfulness, and kindness. These form the foundation of a happiness-building routine.

Gratitude: Shifting Your Focus to Abundance

Gratitude is perhaps the most powerful happiness practice. It works by shifting your attention from what's lacking to what's present, from problems to blessings. Regular gratitude practice has been shown to:

- Increase life satisfaction by 25%
- Improve sleep quality
- Strengthen immune function
- Enhance relationships
- Reduce depression and anxiety

Effective Gratitude Practices:

1. ***The Three Good Things Exercise***: Each evening, write down three things that went well during the day and why you think they happened. This simple practice can increase happiness for months after just one week of practice.

2. *Gratitude Letters*: Write a detailed letter to someone who has positively impacted your life. If possible, deliver and read it in person. This practice creates lasting increases in happiness for both the writer and recipient.
3. *Gratitude Visits*: Regularly visit or call people to express appreciation for specific ways they've helped you.
4. *Mindful Gratitude*: Throughout the day, pause to notice and appreciate small moments—a warm cup of coffee, a friend's smile, a beautiful sunset.

Savoring: Amplifying Positive Experiences

Savoring involves paying deliberate attention to positive experiences to enhance and extend their impact. While gratitude focuses on appreciation, savoring focuses on full engagement with pleasure and joy.

Three Types of Savoring:
1. *Anticipation*: Looking forward to positive events increases happiness before they occur. Plan enjoyable activities and spend time imagining how good they'll be.
2. *Present-Moment Savoring*: During positive experiences, slow down and pay full attention. Notice sensory details, emotions, and thoughts. Share the experience with others when possible.
3. *Reminiscence*: Regularly recall and relive positive memories. Keep a journal of good times, create photo albums, or simply spend time mentally revisiting happy moments.

Mindfulness: Cultivating Present-Moment Awareness

Mindfulness is the practice of paying attention to the present moment without judgment. It increases happiness by reducing rumination, increasing self-awareness, and helping you respond rather than react to life's challenges.

Simple Mindfulness Practices:
1. *Mindful Breathing*: Spend 5-10 minutes daily focusing on your breath. When your mind wanders, gently return attention to breathing.
2. *Body Scan*: Systematically pay attention to different parts of your body, noticing sensations without trying to change them.
3. *Mindful Daily Activities*: Choose routine activities (eating, walking, washing dishes) and do them with full attention.
4. *Loving-Kindness Meditation*: Send thoughts of goodwill to yourself, loved ones, neutral people, difficult people, and all beings.

Kindness: The Happiness Boomerang
Acts of kindness create what researchers call a "helper's high"—performing kind acts increases happiness in the giver, receiver, and even witnesses. Kindness also strengthens social connections and creates positive feedback loops in communities.

Kindness Practices:
1. ***Random Acts of Kindness***: Perform unexpected kind acts for strangers—pay for someone's coffee, help carry groceries, give genuine compliments.
2. ***Planned Kindness***: Intentionally help friends, family, or colleagues in specific ways they would appreciate.
3. ***Self-Kindness***: Treat yourself with the same compassion you'd show a good friend, especially during difficult times.
4. ***Volunteer Service***: Regular volunteering provides structured opportunities for kindness while contributing to causes you care about.

The Kaizen Approach to Happiness Habits

The Japanese principle of Kaizen—continuous improvement through small steps—is perfect for building happiness habits. Rather than trying to transform your entire life overnight, start with tiny changes that feel almost effortlessly manageable.

The 1% Principle
Aim to improve your happiness habits by just 1% each day. This might mean:
- Adding one item to your gratitude list
- Spending one extra minute in mindfulness
- performing one small act of kindness
- Savoring one additional positive moment

These micro-improvements compound over time, creating significant transformation without overwhelming your willpower.

Habit Stacking for Happiness
Attach new happiness habits to existing routines:
- "After I brush my teeth, I will think of three things I'm grateful for"
- "After I sit down for lunch, I will take three mindful breaths"
- "After I check my email, I will send one appreciative message"
- "After I get into bed, I will recall one positive moment from the day"

The Physical Foundation: Exercise, Sleep, and Nutrition
Your physical well-being directly impacts your emotional state. Taking care of your body is one of the most effective ways to support your happiness.

Exercise: Nature's Antidepressant

Regular physical activity is as effective as medication for treating mild to moderate depression and anxiety. Exercise increases endorphins, improves sleep, boosts self-esteem, and provides a sense of accomplishment.

Happiness-Boosting Exercise Guidelines:

Aim for at least 30 minutes of moderate activity most days

Choose activities you enjoy rather than forcing yourself through miserable workouts

Exercise outdoors when possible for additional mood benefits

Include both cardiovascular exercise and strength training

Start small—even a 10-minute walk can improve mood

Sleep: The Foundation of Emotional Regulation

Poor sleep dramatically impacts mood, decision-making, and stress resilience. Quality sleep is essential for processing emotions and maintaining psychological well-being.

Sleep Hygiene for Happiness:
- Maintain consistent sleep and wake times
- Create a relaxing bedtime routine
- Keep your bedroom cool, dark, and quiet
- Avoid screens for at least an hour before bed
- Limit caffeine and alcohol, especially in the evening
- Get natural light exposure during the day

Nutrition: Feeding Your Mood

What you eat affects how you feel. Certain foods support brain health and emotional stability, while others can contribute to mood swings and energy crashes.

Mood-Supporting Nutrition:
- Eat regular, balanced meals to maintain stable blood sugar
- Include omega-3 fatty acids (fish, walnuts, flax seeds)
- Choose complex carbohydrates over simple sugars
- Stay adequately hydrated
- Limit processed foods and excessive caffeine
- Consider the Mediterranean diet pattern, which is linked to better mental health

Social Connection: Why Relationships Matter Most

The Harvard Study of Adult Development, spanning over 80 years, reached a clear conclusion: good relationships keep us happier and healthier. Social connection is so fundamental to well-being that loneliness has health impacts equivalent to smoking 15 cigarettes per day.

Building Meaningful Connections

Quality trumps quantity in relationships. Focus on deepening existing relationships rather than constantly seeking new ones:

- *Practice Active Listening*: Give people your full attention when they speak. Put away devices, make eye contact, and ask thoughtful questions.
- *Share Vulnerably*: Open up about your authentic experiences, including struggles and fears. Vulnerability creates deeper connections.
- *Be Consistently Available*: Show up for people during both good times and bad. Reliability builds trust and strengthens bonds.
- *Express Appreciation*: Regularly tell people what you value about them. Be specific about their positive impact on your life.
- *Create Shared Experiences*: Plan activities that create positive memories together—cooking meals, taking walks, playing games, or pursuing shared interests.

Nurturing Your Social Circle

- *Inner Circle*: Maintain 3-5 very close relationships that provide deep emotional support and intimacy.
- *Middle Circle*: Cultivate 10-15 meaningful friendships that provide companionship, shared interests, and mutual support.
- *Outer Circle*: Maintain friendly connections with colleagues, neighbors, and community members who contribute to your sense of belonging.

Managing Difficult Relationships

Not all relationships contribute to happiness. Some may drain your energy or create stress:

- *Set Boundaries*: Clearly communicate what behavior you will and won't accept.
- *Limit Exposure*: Reduce time spent with consistently negative or toxic people.
- *Practice Compassion*: Try to understand difficult people without absorbing their negativity.
- *Seek Support*: Talk to trusted friends or professionals about challenging relationships.

- ***Know When to Let Go***: Sometimes the healthiest choice is ending relationships that consistently harm your well-being.

Creating Your Personal Happiness Routine

Design a daily routine that incorporates happiness-building practices in a sustainable way:

Morning Routine (10-15 minutes)

Upon waking, think of three things you're grateful for

Set a positive intention for the day

Do 5 minutes of mindful breathing or meditation

Engage in light physical movement

Midday Check-in (5 minutes)

Pause to notice one thing you're enjoying about your day

Take three deep, mindful breaths

Send an appreciative text or email to someone

Step outside for fresh air and natural light

Evening Reflection (10 minutes)

Write in a gratitude journal

Recall and savor one positive moment from the day

Practice loving-kindness meditation

Plan one act of kindness for tomorrow

Weekly Practices

Schedule quality time with loved ones

Engage in a flow-inducing activity

Spend time in nature

Perform volunteer service or help others

Reflect on your values and purpose

Action: Choose One Happiness Habit to Start This Week

Rather than overwhelming yourself with multiple changes, select one happiness habit to focus on for the next week:

Step 1: Choose Your Focus

Select one practice that resonates most with you:

Daily gratitude journaling

Mindful breathing for 5 minutes daily

One act of kindness each day

Savoring one positive experience daily

Taking a 10-minute walk outside

Step 2: Make It Specific

Define exactly when and how you'll practice:

What time of day?

Where will you do it?

How long will it take?

What will trigger the habit?

Step 3: Start Ridiculously Small

Make the habit so easy you can't fail:

Write one sentence of gratitude instead of three pages

Take three mindful breaths instead of meditating for 20 minutes

Hold the door for one person instead of planning elaborate kind acts

Step 4: Track Your Progress

Use a simple method to monitor consistency:

Check off days on a calendar

Use a habit-tracking app

Keep a brief journal of your experience

Step 5: Celebrate Success

Acknowledge your efforts and progress:

Celebrate completing each day

Notice any changes in your mood or outlook

Share your success with a supportive friend

Remember, the goal is consistency, not perfection. Even practicing your chosen habit 4-5 days out of 7 will create positive changes over time. Once this habit feels natural, you can add another one using the same process.

Chapter 4 – Mindset Shifts for a Happier Life

Your mindset—the lens through which you view yourself, others, and the world—profoundly impacts your happiness. This chapter explores how shifting your mental patterns can transform your experience of life, even when external circumstances remain unchanged.

Fixed vs. Growth Mindset and Their Impact on Happiness

Stanford psychologist Carol Dweck's research on mindset reveals how our beliefs about our abilities fundamentally shape our experience. This has profound implications for happiness and well-being[2].

Fixed Mindset: The Happiness Trap

People with a fixed mindset believe that qualities like intelligence, talent, and personality are static traits that can't be significantly developed. This creates several barriers to happiness:

1. *Fear of Failure*: When you believe abilities are fixed, failure feels like a judgment of your worth rather than information for improvement.
2. *Perfectionism*: Fixed mindset individuals often avoid challenges to protect their self-image, missing opportunities for growth and satisfaction.
3. *Comparison Trap*: When abilities seem fixed, others' success can feel threatening rather than inspiring.
4. *Learned Helplessness*: Setbacks feel permanent and personal, leading to resignation rather than resilience.

Growth Mindset: The Path to Resilient Happiness

People with a growth mindset believe that abilities can be developed through effort, learning, and persistence. This creates multiple pathways to happiness:

1. *Embracing Challenges*: Difficulties become opportunities for growth rather than threats to self-worth.
2. *Learning from Failure*: Setbacks provide valuable information rather than evidence of inadequacy.
3. *Finding Joy in Process*: The journey of improvement becomes satisfying, not just the destination.
4. *Celebrating Others' Success*: Others' achievements become sources of inspiration and learning rather than comparison and envy.

Cultivating a Growth Mindset for Happiness
1. **Reframe Challenges**: Instead of "This is too hard," think "This will help me grow."
2. **Embrace the Power of "Yet"**: Replace "I can't do this" with "I can't do this yet."
3. **Focus on Process**: Celebrate effort, strategy, and progress rather than just outcomes.
4. **Learn from Criticism**: View feedback as valuable information rather than personal attack.
5. **Find Lessons in Setbacks**: Ask "What can I learn from this?" rather than "Why me?"

Reframing Negative Thoughts and Practicing Self-Compassion
Your inner dialogue significantly impacts your happiness. Learning to recognize and reframe negative thought patterns while treating yourself with compassion can dramatically improve your well-being.

Common Negative Thought Patterns
- **All-or-Nothing Thinking**: Seeing situations in black and white terms
  "I completely failed" instead of "I made some mistakes but also did some things well"

- **Mental Filter**: Focusing exclusively on negative aspects while ignoring positives
  Dwelling on one criticism while dismissing multiple compliments

- **Jumping to Conclusions**: Making negative assumptions without evidence
  "They didn't respond to my text, so they must be angry with me"

- **Catastrophizing**: Imagining the worst possible outcomes
  "If I don't get this job, my career is over"

- **Personalization**: Taking responsibility for things outside your control
  "The meeting went badly because I didn't prepare enough" (when multiple factors were involved)

The ABCDE Method for Reframing
Developed by psychologist Martin Seligman, this method helps you challenge and change negative thoughts:

A - Adversity: Identify the triggering event or situation

B - Beliefs: Notice the automatic thoughts and beliefs about the situation

C - Consequences: Observe the emotional and behavioral results of these beliefs

D - Disputation: Challenge the negative beliefs by asking:
- Is this thought accurate?
- Is it helpful?
- What evidence supports or contradicts it?
- What would I tell a friend in this situation?
- What's a more balanced perspective?

E - Energization: Notice how you feel after reframing the thought

Example of ABCDE in Action:

A - Adversity: Your presentation at work didn't go as well as planned

B - Beliefs: "I'm terrible at presentations. Everyone thinks I'm incompetent."

C - Consequences: Feeling anxious, avoiding future presentation opportunities

D - Disputation:
- "Is this completely true? I've given successful presentations before."
- "What evidence do I have that everyone thinks I'm incompetent? Several colleagues offered helpful feedback."
- "What would I tell a friend? That one presentation doesn't define their abilities."

E - Energization: Feeling more balanced and motivated to improve for next time

The Practice of Self-Compassion

Self-compassion involves treating yourself with the same kindness you'd show a good friend, especially during difficult times. Research shows that self-compassionate people are happier, more resilient, and less anxious.

Three Components of Self-Compassion:
1. *Self-Kindness vs. Self-Judgment*: Being warm and understanding toward yourself when you suffer or fail, rather than harsh and critical.
2. *Common Humanity vs. Isolation*: Recognizing that suffering and failure are part of the shared human experience, rather than feeling isolated in your struggles.
3. *Mindfulness vs. Over-Identification*: Holding your thoughts and feelings in mindful awareness rather than being swept away by them.

Self-Compassion Practices:

The Self-Compassion Break: When facing difficulty, place your hand on your heart and say:
- "This is a moment of suffering" (mindfulness)

- "Suffering is part of life" (common humanity)
- "May I be kind to myself" (self-kindness)

Self-Compassionate Letter Writing: Write yourself a letter from the perspective of a loving, wise friend who understands your struggles and offers comfort and encouragement.

Loving-Kindness for Self: Practice sending yourself the same loving wishes you'd send to others:
- "May I be happy, may I be healthy, may I be at peace."
- Letting Go of Comparison, Perfectionism, and "Destination Addiction"
- Three mental patterns particularly undermine happiness: comparison with others, perfectionism, and believing happiness lies in some future achievement.
- Breaking Free from Comparison
- Social comparison is natural but often destructive in our social media age. Constant comparison with others' highlight reels creates dissatisfaction with your own life.

Strategies for Reducing Comparison:
- *Limit Social Media*: Reduce time on platforms that trigger comparison, or curate your feeds to include more authentic, diverse content.
- *Practice Gratitude*: Regularly appreciate what you have rather than focusing on what others appear to have.
- *Focus on Your Journey*: Compare yourself to who you were yesterday, not to others today.
- *Celebrate Others*: When you notice comparison arising, consciously celebrate others' success instead of resenting it.
- *Remember the Iceberg*: What you see of others' lives is usually just the tip of the iceberg—everyone faces struggles you don't see.

Overcoming Perfectionism

Perfectionism masquerades as a virtue but often creates anxiety, procrastination, and dissatisfaction. Healthy striving differs from perfectionism in important ways:
- *Perfectionism*: "I must do this flawlessly or I'm a failure"
  Healthy Striving: "I want to do my best and learn from the experience"
- *Perfectionism*: Focuses on avoiding mistakes
  Healthy Striving: Focuses on growth and improvement
- *Perfectionism*: All-or-nothing thinking
  Healthy Striving: Recognizes progress and partial success

Anti-Perfectionism Strategies:
- ***Set "Good Enough" Standards***: For most tasks, identify what constitutes "good enough" and stop there.
- ***Embrace "Done is Better Than Perfect"***: Complete projects at 80% rather than endlessly refining them.
- ***Practice Deliberate Imperfection***: Intentionally do some things imperfectly to build tolerance for mistakes.
- ***Celebrate Progress***: Acknowledge improvement and effort, not just perfect outcomes.
- ***Learn from Mistakes***: View errors as valuable learning opportunities rather than failures.

Curing "Destination Addiction"

Destination addiction is the belief that happiness exists somewhere else—in the future, in different circumstances, or in achieving specific goals. This mindset keeps happiness perpetually out of reach.

Common Destination Addiction Thoughts:
- "I'll be happy when I get promoted"
- "I'll be happy when I lose weight"
- "I'll be happy when I find the right relationship"
- "I'll be happy when I retire"

Strategies for Present-Moment Happiness:
- ***Practice Gratitude for Now***: Regularly appreciate what's good about your current situation.
- ***Find Joy in the Journey***: Look for satisfaction in the process of pursuing goals, not just achieving them.
- ***Set Process Goals***: Focus on actions you can take today rather than just outcome goals.
- ***Celebrate Small Wins***: Acknowledge progress and minor achievements along the way.
- ***Mindful Presence***: Regularly bring your attention to the present moment and find something to appreciate.

The Power of Acceptance and Resilience

Acceptance doesn't mean passive resignation—it means acknowledging reality without wasting energy fighting what you cannot change. This creates space for effective action and emotional peace.

The Serenity Prayer Principle

"Grant me the serenity to accept the things I cannot change, the courage to change the things I can, and the wisdom to know the difference."

This principle helps you direct your energy toward what you can influence while finding peace with what you cannot.

What You Can Control:
- Your thoughts and interpretations
- Your actions and behaviors
- Your responses to events
- Your habits and routines
- Your goals and priorities
- Your relationships and boundaries

What You Cannot Control:
- Other people's actions and choices
- Past events
- Future outcomes
- Natural disasters and accidents
- Aging and death
- Economic conditions and politics

Building Resilience Through Acceptance

- ***Acknowledge Difficult Emotions***: Allow yourself to feel sadness, anger, or disappointment without judgment.
- ***Practice Radical Acceptance***: When facing unchangeable situations, consciously choose to accept them rather than fighting reality.
- ***Focus on Response***: Ask "Given this situation, what's my best response?" rather than "Why is this happening to me?"
- ***Find Meaning in Adversity***: Look for lessons, growth opportunities, or ways to help others through your experiences.

- **Build Your Support Network**: Cultivate relationships that provide comfort and perspective during difficult times.

Action: Mindset Reframing and Self-Talk Exercise

This exercise helps you identify and transform negative thought patterns that undermine your happiness:

Step 1: Thought Awareness (Week 1)

For one week, simply notice your self-talk without trying to change it. Carry a small notebook or use your phone to record:
- Negative thoughts about yourself
- Pessimistic predictions about the future
- Harsh self-criticism
- Comparison thoughts
- Perfectionist demands

Step 2: Pattern Recognition (End of Week 1)

Review your notes and identify patterns:
- What situations trigger negative self-talk?
- What themes appear repeatedly?
- Which cognitive distortions do you use most?
- How do these thoughts make you feel?

Step 3: Thought Challenging (Week 2)

For each negative thought you notice, ask:
- Is this thought completely accurate?
- What evidence supports or contradicts it?
- What would I tell a friend thinking this way?
- What's a more balanced perspective?
- How would thinking differently change how I feel?

Step 4: Replacement Thoughts (Week 3)

Create more balanced, realistic alternatives to your common negative thoughts:

Original: "I always mess things up" **Replacement**: "I make mistakes sometimes, like everyone, and I can learn from them"

Original: "I'm not good enough" **Replacement**: "I'm growing and improving, and I have many valuable qualities"

Original: "This will never work out" **Replacement**: "I don't know how this will turn out, but I can handle whatever happens"

Step 5: Self-Compassion Practice (Week 4)

When you notice self-criticism, immediately practice self-compassion:

- Acknowledge the difficulty: "This is hard right now"
- Remember common humanity: "Everyone struggles sometimes"
- Offer yourself kindness: "May I be gentle with myself"

Step 6: Daily Affirmations (Ongoing)

Create personal affirmations based on your growth mindset and self-compassion work:

- "I am capable of learning and growing"
- "I treat myself with kindness and understanding"
- "I focus on progress, not perfection"
- "I am worthy of love and happiness"

Practice these affirmations daily, especially during challenging times.

Step 7: Progress Review (Monthly)

Each month, review your progress:

- Which negative thought patterns have decreased?
- How has your self-talk changed?
- What impact have you noticed on your mood and behavior?
- What areas still need work?

Remember, changing thought patterns takes time and practice. Be patient with yourself as you develop these new mental habits. The goal isn't to eliminate all negative thoughts but to respond to them more skillfully and maintain a more balanced, compassionate inner dialogue.

Chapter 5 – Overcoming Obstacles: When Happiness Feels Out of Reach

Even with the best intentions and practices, there will be times when happiness feels elusive or impossible. This chapter addresses the common obstacles that can derail your well-being and provides practical strategies for navigating difficult periods while maintaining your commitment to a fulfilling life.

The "Happiness Traps": Materialism, Busyness, and External Validation

Modern culture presents several seductive but ultimately counterproductive paths to happiness. Recognizing these traps is the first step to avoiding them.

The Materialism Trap

Consumer culture promises that the next purchase will bring lasting satisfaction. This creates a cycle where people constantly seek happiness through acquisition, only to find that material gains provide temporary pleasure at best.

Why Materialism Undermines Happiness:

- Creates endless comparison with others' possessions
- Shifts focus from relationships and experiences to objects
- Promotes debt and financial stress
- Leads to adaptation—new purchases quickly feel normal
- Emphasizes external status over internal satisfaction

Breaking Free from Materialism:

- **Practice Gratitude for What You Have**: Regularly appreciate your current possessions rather than focusing on what you lack.
- **Invest in Experiences Over Things**: Research shows experiences provide more lasting happiness than material purchases.
- **Buy Time, Not Stuff**: When possible, purchase services that give you more time for relationships and meaningful activities.
- **Practice Voluntary Simplicity**: Consciously choose to live with less, focusing on quality over quantity.
- **Delay Gratification**: Wait 24-48 hours before making non-essential purchases to ensure they align with your values.

The Busyness Trap

Many people equate busyness with importance and productivity with worth. This creates a culture where being overwhelmed is seen as a badge of honor, but constant busyness actually undermines happiness and effectiveness.

How Busyness Destroys Happiness:

- Prevents deep engagement with meaningful activities
- Reduces time for relationships and self-care
- Creates chronic stress and anxiety
- Eliminates space for reflection and growth
- Leads to decision fatigue and poor choices

Escaping the Busyness Trap:

- **Distinguish Urgent from Important**: Use the Eisenhower Matrix to focus on what truly matters rather than what feels pressing.
- **Practice Saying No**: Protect your time and energy by declining commitments that don't align with your values and priorities.
- **Schedule Downtime**: Treat rest and relaxation as essential appointments, not optional activities.
- **Single-Task**: Focus on one activity at a time rather than multitasking, which reduces both effectiveness and satisfaction.
- **Create Boundaries**: Establish clear limits between work and personal time, especially in our always-connected world.

The External Validation Trap

Seeking happiness through others' approval creates a fragile foundation for well-being. When your self-worth depends on external validation, you become vulnerable to others' opinions and lose touch with your authentic self.

Signs You're Trapped by External Validation:

- Constantly seeking compliments and reassurance
- Feeling anxious when others don't respond positively
- Making decisions based on what others will think
- Comparing your achievements to others'
- Feeling empty despite external success

Building Internal Validation:

- **Identify Your Core Values**: Make decisions based on your principles rather than others' expectations.

- **Practice Self-Appreciation**: Regularly acknowledge your efforts, progress, and positive qualities.
- **Seek Feedback, Not Approval**: Ask for specific input to improve rather than general validation.
- **Celebrate Private Victories**: Find satisfaction in personal growth that others may not notice.
- **Surround Yourself with Authentic People**: Build relationships with those who appreciate your true self.

Navigating Sadness, Stress, and Disappointment

Happiness is not the absence of negative emotions—it's the ability to experience the full range of human feelings without being overwhelmed by them. Learning to navigate difficult emotions skillfully is essential for lasting well-being.

Understanding the Purpose of Negative Emotions

Negative emotions serve important functions:
- **Sadness** helps us process loss and signals the need for support
- **Anger** alerts us to injustice and motivates action
- **Fear** protects us from danger and helps us prepare for challenges
- **Disappointment** provides information about unmet expectations
- **Anxiety** helps us anticipate and prepare for future threats

The goal isn't to eliminate these emotions but to respond to them wisely.

The RAIN Technique for Difficult Emotions

This mindfulness-based approach helps you navigate challenging feelings:
- **R - Recognize**: Notice what you're feeling without immediately trying to change it. "I notice I'm feeling anxious right now."
- **A - Allow**: Give yourself permission to feel the emotion without judgment. "It's okay to feel this way."
- **I - Investigate**: Explore the emotion with curiosity. Where do you feel it in your body? What thoughts accompany it? What might it be telling you?
- **N - Nurture**: Offer yourself compassion and care. What do you need right now? How can you comfort yourself?

Healthy Strategies for Common Difficult Emotions

For Sadness:
- Allow yourself to grieve and feel the emotion fully
- Seek support from trusted friends or family
- Engage in gentle, nurturing activities
- Express your feelings through journaling or creative outlets
- Remember that sadness is temporary and serves a purpose

For Anger:
- Take time to cool down before responding
- Identify what boundary or value has been violated
- Express your feelings assertively, not aggressively
- Channel anger into constructive action when appropriate
- Practice forgiveness when ready, for your own peace

For Anxiety:
- Use grounding techniques to return to the present moment
- Challenge catastrophic thinking with realistic assessments
- Break overwhelming tasks into smaller, manageable steps
- Practice relaxation techniques like deep breathing
- Seek professional help if anxiety becomes overwhelming

For Disappointment:
- Acknowledge and validate your feelings
- Examine whether your expectations were realistic
- Look for lessons or growth opportunities
- Adjust your approach or goals if necessary
- Practice acceptance of outcomes beyond your control

The Role of Forgiveness and Letting Go of Grudges

Holding onto resentment is like drinking poison and expecting the other person to get sick. Forgiveness is not about excusing harmful behavior—it's about freeing yourself from the burden of anger and resentment.

Understanding Forgiveness

Forgiveness is:
- A choice to release resentment for your own well-being
- A process that takes time, not a one-time event

- About your internal state, not the other person's behavior
- Compatible with setting boundaries and seeking justice
- A gift you give yourself, not the person who hurt you

Forgiveness is not:
- Excusing or minimizing harmful behavior
- Forgetting what happened
- Automatically trusting the person again
- Avoiding consequences for harmful actions
- Required if you're not ready

The Forgiveness Process
- ***Step 1: Acknowledge the Hurt.*** Recognize and validate the pain you've experienced. Don't minimize or dismiss your feelings.
- ***Step 2: Feel Your Emotions.*** Allow yourself to experience anger, sadness, or disappointment fully. These emotions are valid and important.
- ***Step 3: Choose to Forgive.*** Make a conscious decision to begin the forgiveness process for your own well-being, not for the other person.
- ***Step 4: Reframe the Experience.*** Look for lessons, growth opportunities, or ways the experience has made you stronger or wiser.
- ***Step 5: Release the Resentment.*** Consciously let go of the desire for revenge or punishment. This may need to be repeated many times.
- ***Step 6: Wish the Person Well.*** Eventually, you may be able to genuinely hope for the other person's happiness and growth.

Self-Forgiveness
Often the hardest person to forgive is yourself. Self-forgiveness follows a similar process:
- Acknowledge your mistakes without minimizing them
- Take responsibility for your actions
- Make amends when possible and appropriate
- Learn from the experience
- Commit to doing better in the future
- Practice self-compassion and let go of self-punishment

Coping with Setbacks: Bounce-Back Strategies and Support Systems

Resilience—the ability to bounce back from adversity—is a crucial component of lasting happiness. While some people seem naturally resilient, these skills can be developed by anyone.

Building Resilience

- ***Develop a Growth Mindset***: View setbacks as opportunities to learn and grow rather than evidence of failure.
- ***Cultivate Optimism***: Look for silver linings and possibilities even in difficult situations.
- ***Build Strong Relationships***: Maintain connections with people who provide emotional support and practical help.
- ***Practice Self-Care***: Take care of your physical and emotional needs, especially during stressful times.
- ***Find Meaning in Adversity***: Look for ways your struggles can help you grow or help others.
- ***Maintain Perspective***: Remember that most setbacks are temporary and don't define your entire life.

The Bounce-Back Process

When facing a significant setback:

- ***Step 1: Allow Initial Reactions.*** Give yourself time to feel disappointed, angry, or sad. Don't rush to "get over it."
- ***Step 2: Assess the Situation.*** Once the initial emotional intensity subsides, objectively evaluate what happened and what you can learn.
- ***Step 3: Identify What You Can Control.*** Focus your energy on aspects of the situation you can influence rather than what's beyond your control.
- ***Step 4: Create an Action Plan.*** Develop specific steps to address the situation or prevent similar problems in the future.
- ***Step 5: Seek Support.*** Reach out to friends, family, mentors, or professionals who can provide guidance and encouragement.
- ***Step 6: Take Action.*** Begin implementing your plan, starting with small, manageable steps.
- ***Step 7: Practice Self-Compassion.*** Be patient with yourself as you recover and rebuild. Healing takes time.

Building Your Support System

A strong support network is essential for navigating difficult times:

- ***Emotional Support***: People who listen, empathize, and provide comfort during tough times.
- ***Practical Support***: Those who can help with concrete tasks or resources when you're overwhelmed.

- ***Informational Support***: Individuals who can provide advice, guidance, or expertise relevant to your challenges.
- ***Social Support***: Friends and family who provide a sense of belonging and connection.
- ***Professional Support***: Therapists, coaches, or counselors who can provide specialized help when needed.

Action: Forgiveness or Letting-Go Letter

This exercise helps you process difficult emotions and move toward forgiveness or acceptance:

Step 1: Choose Your Focus. Identify someone you need to forgive (including yourself) or a situation you need to let go of.

Step 2: Write Freely. Write a letter expressing all your thoughts and feelings about the situation. Don't censor yourself—this is for your eyes only. Include:
- What happened and how it affected you
- Your emotions about the situation
- What you wish had been different
- How the situation has impacted your life
- What you've learned from the experience

Step 3: Express Your Feelings. Allow yourself to feel whatever emotions arise as you write. This might include anger, sadness, disappointment, or relief.

Step 4: Shift Toward Release. In the second part of your letter, focus on letting go:
- Acknowledge that holding onto resentment hurts you more than anyone else
- Express your intention to forgive or let go for your own well-being
- Identify any lessons or growth that came from the experience
- If appropriate, express hope for the other person's growth and happiness

Step 5: Ritual of Release. Choose a symbolic way to release the letter and your resentment:
- Burn the letter safely (representing transformation)
- Bury it in the ground (representing letting go)
- Tear it up and throw it away (representing disposal of old pain)
- Keep it and read it periodically to track your healing progress

Step 6: Follow-Up Actions. Consider what additional steps might support your healing:
- Having a conversation with the person (if safe and appropriate)
- Seeking professional counseling

- Making amends if you've hurt someone
- Setting new boundaries to protect yourself
- Engaging in activities that bring you joy and peace

Step 7: Practice Patience. Remember that forgiveness is a process, not a one-time event. You may need to choose forgiveness repeatedly as old feelings resurface. This is normal and doesn't mean you're failing.

This exercise can be repeated whenever you face new hurts or when old resentments resurface. The goal is not to forget what happened but to free yourself from the burden of carrying anger and resentment.

Chapter 6 – Designing a Life that Supports Happiness

Creating lasting happiness requires more than positive thinking and good intentions—it demands intentionally designing your life to support well-being. This chapter explores how to align your daily existence with your values, strengths, and deepest sources of meaning.

Aligning Your Daily Life with Your Values and Strengths

True happiness emerges when your life reflects your authentic self. This means understanding your core values and natural strengths, then structuring your days to honor both.

Discovering Your Core Values

Values are your fundamental beliefs about what's important in life. They serve as your internal compass, guiding decisions and providing a sense of direction. When your actions align with your values, you experience greater satisfaction and authenticity[2].

Common Core Values Categories:

- **Relationship Values**: Family, friendship, love, community, service to others
- **Achievement Values**: Success, recognition, mastery, competition, influence
- **Security Values**: Stability, financial security, health, safety, tradition
- **Growth Values**: Learning, creativity, adventure, personal development, spirituality
- **Freedom Values**: Independence, autonomy, flexibility, travel, self-expression

Values Clarification Exercise:

From a comprehensive list of values, select your top 10

Narrow these down to your top 5 core values

Rank these 5 in order of importance

For each value, write a brief description of what it means to you

Identify specific ways you currently honor or neglect each value

Living Your Values Daily

Once you've identified your core values, the challenge is integrating them into your daily life:

- **Decision-Making Filter**: Before making important decisions, ask "Does this align with my core values?"
- **Daily Value Check-In**: Each evening, reflect on how well your day honored your values.

- **Value-Based Goals**: Ensure your major goals support rather than conflict with your values.
- **Boundary Setting**: Use your values to determine what you will and won't accept in relationships and commitments.
- **Career Alignment**: Seek work that allows you to express your values, even if it means making trade-offs.

Identifying and Leveraging Your Strengths

Your strengths are the talents, skills, and characteristics that energize you and come naturally. Research shows that people who use their strengths regularly are more engaged, productive, and happy.

Types of Strengths:

- **Character Strengths**: Core virtues like courage, wisdom, justice, and temperance
- **Talent Strengths**: Natural abilities in areas like communication, analysis, or creativity
- **Learned Strengths**: Skills developed through practice and experience
- **Relationship Strengths**: Abilities in connecting with and influencing others

Strengths Discovery Methods:

- **Reflection**: What activities make you feel most alive and energized?
- **Feedback**: What do others consistently praise you for?
- **Performance**: What tasks do you complete easily while others struggle?
- **Learning**: What skills do you pick up quickly?
- **Satisfaction**: What accomplishments give you the deepest sense of pride?

Maximizing Your Strengths

- **Strength-Based Role Design**: Shape your job responsibilities to emphasize your strengths
- **Complementary Partnerships**: Team up with people whose strengths complement yours
- **Strength Development**: Invest time in developing your top strengths rather than fixing weaknesses
- **Strength Application**: Look for new ways to apply your strengths in different contexts
- **Strength Sharing**: Teach others and mentor them in areas where you excel

The Importance of Purpose, Meaning, and Contribution

Purpose provides the "why" behind your actions, giving your life direction and significance. People with a strong sense of purpose report higher levels of happiness, better health, and greater resilience.

Understanding Purpose vs. Passion

Purpose is broader and more stable—it's about the impact you want to have and the legacy you want to leave.

Passion is more specific and can change—it's about activities and interests that excite you.

Your purpose might be "helping others reach their potential," which could be expressed through various passions like teaching, coaching, parenting, or mentoring.

Finding Your Purpose

The Intersection Method: Your purpose often lies at the intersection of:
- What you're good at (your strengths)
- What you love doing (your passions)
- What the world needs (problems you care about solving)
- What you can be paid for (if relevant to your career)

The Legacy Question: How do you want to be remembered? What impact do you want to have on others?

The Anger Method: What problems in the world make you angry or sad? These often point toward your purpose.

The Childhood Dreams Method: What did you want to be when you grew up? The underlying themes often reveal purpose.

The Peak Experience Method: When have you felt most fulfilled and alive? What were you doing?

Creating Meaning in Daily Life

Even mundane activities can become meaningful when connected to larger purposes:
- **Reframe Your Work**: Connect your job tasks to their impact on others or larger goals
- **Serve Others**: Look for ways to help, support, or contribute to others' well-being
- **Personal Growth**: View challenges as opportunities to develop character and wisdom

- **_Legacy Building_**: Consider how your actions today contribute to the legacy you want to leave
- **_Connection Creation_**: Use daily interactions to build relationships and community

The Ripple Effect of Contribution

Contributing to something larger than yourself creates multiple benefits:

- Provides perspective during personal struggles
- Creates a sense of significance and worth
- Builds connections with like-minded people
- Develops empathy and compassion

Chapter 7 – The Ripple Effect

How Your Happiness Impacts Others

Your happiness is not a selfish pursuit—it's a gift to everyone around you. Research reveals that emotions are contagious, spreading through families, workplaces, and communities like ripples in a pond. When you cultivate genuine well-being, you create positive change that extends far beyond yourself.

The Science of Emotional Contagion

Emotional contagion is the phenomenon where people unconsciously mimic and "catch" the emotions of those around them. This happens through multiple mechanisms:

Mirror Neurons: These specialized brain cells fire both when you perform an action and when you observe someone else performing the same action. They help you understand and empathize with others' emotions.

Facial Mimicry: We unconsciously mirror others' facial expressions, which then influences our own emotional state through the facial feedback hypothesis.

Vocal Synchrony: People naturally adjust their tone, pace, and energy to match those they're interacting with.

Physiological Synchronization: Heart rates, breathing patterns, and stress hormones can synchronize between people in close proximity.

Research Findings on Happiness Contagion

The Framingham Heart Study, which tracked social networks for decades, found that:

- Having a happy friend who lives within a mile increases your probability of happiness by 25%
- A happy spouse increases your happiness probability by 8%
- Happy siblings increase your happiness by 14%
- Even friends of friends can influence your happiness

This research demonstrates that happiness spreads through social networks up to three degrees of separation—meaning your happiness can positively impact people you've never even met.

How Happiness Enhances Relationships

Happy people are more attractive as friends, partners, and colleagues because happiness enhances the qualities that make relationships thrive:

Increased Empathy and Compassion

When you're in a positive emotional state, you're more likely to:
- Notice others' needs and emotions
- Respond with kindness and understanding
- Offer help and support spontaneously
- See the best in people rather than focusing on their flaws

Better Communication Skills

Happiness improves your ability to:
- Listen actively without being defensive
- Express yourself clearly and positively
- Resolve conflicts constructively
- Give and receive feedback gracefully

Enhanced Generosity and Kindness

Research shows that happy people are more likely to:
- Volunteer their time for causes they care about
- Donate money to charity
- Help strangers in need
- Perform random acts of kindness

Greater Emotional Stability

Happy individuals provide more stable, supportive relationships because they:
- React less dramatically to stress and setbacks
- Maintain perspective during difficult times
- Offer consistent emotional support to others
- Create a sense of safety and security in relationships

The Link Between Happiness and Leadership

Happy leaders are more effective because their positive emotions enhance their ability to inspire, motivate, and guide others.

Characteristics of Happy Leaders

Inspirational Vision: Happy leaders can envision and communicate positive futures that motivate others to work toward shared goals.

Resilient Problem-Solving: They approach challenges with creativity and optimism, finding solutions rather than dwelling on problems.

Authentic Connection: Happy leaders build genuine relationships with their team members, creating trust and loyalty.

Positive Team Culture: They create environments where people feel valued, supported, and encouraged to do their best work.

Effective Decision-Making: Positive emotions broaden thinking and improve judgment, leading to better strategic decisions.

The Happiness Advantage in Leadership
Research by Shawn Achor reveals that happy leaders:
- Have teams that are 31% more productive
- Experience 37% better sales performance
- Are three times more creative in problem-solving
- Have 10 times more engagement from their team members
- Create organizations with lower turnover and higher customer satisfaction

Building a Culture of Happiness
Whether in your family, workplace, or community, you can actively create environments that support and amplify happiness.

In Your Family
Model Positive Emotions: Children learn more from what they observe than what they're told. Demonstrate gratitude, optimism, and resilience.

Create Positive Traditions: Establish family rituals that celebrate connection, gratitude, and joy—weekly appreciation dinners, gratitude journals, or service projects.

Encourage Individual Strengths: Help each family member identify and develop their unique talents and interests.

Practice Forgiveness: Create a family culture where mistakes are learning opportunities and forgiveness is freely given.

Prioritize Relationships: Make time for meaningful conversations, shared activities, and individual attention for each family member.

In Your Workplace

Express Genuine Appreciation: Regularly acknowledge colleagues' contributions and efforts, being specific about their positive impact.

Share Positive News: Celebrate successes, milestones, and good news, both personal and professional.

Create Connection Opportunities: Organize team lunches, coffee breaks, or social events that build relationships beyond work tasks.

Practice Active Listening: Give colleagues your full attention during conversations, showing that you value their thoughts and feelings.

Offer Support: Be available to help others during challenging times, whether with work tasks or personal struggles.

In Your Community

Volunteer for Causes You Care About: Contributing to your community creates connections and provides a sense of purpose.

Practice Random Kindness: Small acts of kindness—holding doors, helping with groceries, offering compliments—create positive ripples.

Support Local Businesses: Build relationships with local business owners and express appreciation for their contributions to the community.

Participate in Community Events: Attend local festivals, meetings, or gatherings to build connections with neighbors.

Share Your Skills: Offer to teach, mentor, or help others develop abilities in areas where you excel.

The Multiplier Effect of Happiness

When you invest in your own happiness, you create what researchers call a "multiplier effect"—your well-being amplifies the positive impact you can have on others.

Personal Energy and Availability

Happy people have more emotional energy to invest in relationships and causes they care about. When you're not depleted by negative emotions, you can:
- Be more present and attentive to others
- Offer support during difficult times
- Engage more fully in activities and conversations

- Maintain consistency in your positive impact

Increased Influence and Persuasion
Positive emotions make you more influential because:
- People are naturally drawn to positive, optimistic individuals
- Happy people are more trusted and seen as credible
- Positive emotions are associated with competence and success
- Others want to be around people who make them feel good

Enhanced Creativity and Problem-Solving
Happy individuals can contribute more effectively to group efforts because:
- Positive emotions broaden thinking and increase creativity
- Happy people are more likely to see opportunities and solutions
- They approach challenges with confidence and persistence
- Their optimism inspires others to think bigger and try harder

Overcoming Happiness Guilt
Some people feel guilty about pursuing happiness, believing it's selfish or that they don't deserve to be happy while others suffer. This guilt actually prevents you from making your maximum positive contribution to the world.

Reframing Happiness as Service
Consider these perspectives:
- Your happiness gives you more energy to help others
- Happy people are more generous and compassionate
- You model possibility for others who are struggling
- Your positive emotions literally improve others' well-being through emotional contagion
- You can't give what you don't have—cultivating happiness allows you to share it

The Oxygen Mask Principle
Just as airplane safety instructions tell you to put on your own oxygen mask before helping others, you must take care of your own well-being before you can effectively support others. This isn't selfish—it's strategic.

Action: Spread Happiness Challenge

This 30-day challenge helps you experience firsthand how your happiness impacts others:

Week 1: Awareness
- Day 1-2: Notice how your mood affects others. Pay attention to how people respond to you when you're happy versus when you're stressed or sad.
- Day 3-4: Observe emotional contagion in action. Watch how emotions spread in your family, workplace, or social groups.
- Day 5-7: Practice mood regulation. When you notice negative emotions, use your happiness tools (gratitude, mindfulness, reframing) to shift your state before interacting with others.

Week 2: Intentional Positivity
- Day 8-10: Start each day with a positive intention. Decide how you want to show up emotionally and commit to maintaining that state.
- Day 11-12: Practice positive greetings. Greet everyone you encounter with genuine warmth and enthusiasm.
- Day 13-14: Share good news. When something positive happens, share it with others to amplify the joy.

Week 3: Active Spreading
- Day 15-17: Give genuine compliments. Offer at least three specific, sincere compliments each day.
- Day 18-19: Practice gratitude expression. Thank people for their contributions, both big and small.
- Day 20-21: Perform random acts of kindness. Do something nice for someone without expecting anything in return.

Week 4: Sustained Impact
- Day 22-24: Create positive traditions. Start a new ritual that brings joy to your family, team, or friend group.
- Day 25-26: Mentor or encourage someone. Share your knowledge or offer support to someone who could benefit.
- Day 27-30: Reflect and commit. Evaluate the impact of your happiness on others and commit to continuing the practices that work best.

Daily Tracking Questions:
- How did my emotional state affect others today?
- What positive impact did I have on someone?
- How did spreading happiness make me feel?
- What did I learn about the connection between my well-being and others'?

Chapter 8 – The 30-Day Happiness Challenge

Knowledge without action remains merely potential. This chapter provides a structured, day-by-day program to transform your understanding of happiness into lasting habits that create genuine well-being.

The Kaizen Approach to Happiness Habits

The 30-Day Happiness Challenge is built on the Japanese principle of Kaizen—continuous improvement through small, manageable steps. Rather than attempting dramatic life changes that often fail, this approach focuses on tiny daily practices that compound over time.

Why Small Steps Work

Reduced Resistance: Small changes don't trigger the brain's resistance to change, making them easier to maintain.

Sustainable Progress: Tiny habits are more likely to stick because they don't require massive willpower or life disruption.

Compound Effect: Small improvements accumulate over time, creating significant transformation.

Confidence Building: Success with small changes builds confidence for larger transformations.

Neural Pathway Development: Repetition of small actions strengthens the neural pathways associated with happiness habits.

The Five Pillars of the Challenge

Each day of the challenge incorporates practices from five core areas that research shows are most effective for building lasting happiness:

Pillar 1: Gratitude and Appreciation. Daily practices that shift your focus from what's lacking to what's abundant in your life.

Pillar 2: Mindfulness and Presence. Techniques to anchor you in the present moment and reduce anxiety about the past or future.

Pillar 3: Connection and Kindness. Activities that strengthen relationships and create positive interactions with others.

Pillar 4: Growth and Meaning. Practices that connect you to your purpose and support personal development.

Pillar 5: Self-Care and Well-Being. Physical and emotional care practices that support your overall health and energy.

Week 1: Foundation Building (Days 1-7)

The first week focuses on establishing basic happiness habits and creating awareness of your current patterns.

Day 1: Happiness Baseline Assessment

Morning Practice: Complete a comprehensive happiness assessment to establish your starting point.

Daily Practice: Begin a gratitude journal—write down three things you're grateful for and why.

Evening Reflection: Rate your overall mood and energy level on a scale of 1-10.

Mindfulness Moment: Take five conscious breaths before each meal.

Day 2: Mindful Morning

Morning Practice: Spend 5 minutes in mindful breathing or meditation.

Daily Practice: Continue gratitude journaling.

Evening Reflection: Notice one moment during the day when you felt fully present.

Connection Practice: Send a text expressing appreciation to someone you care about.

Day 3: Kindness Focus

Morning Practice: Set an intention to perform one act of kindness today.

Daily Practice: Gratitude journaling + perform your planned act of kindness.

Evening Reflection: Write about how the act of kindness made you feel.

Self-Care Practice: Take a 10-minute walk outside.

Day 4: Savoring Practice
Morning Practice: Identify one experience you want to fully savor today.

Daily Practice: Gratitude journaling + practice savoring your chosen experience.

Evening Reflection: Describe the savoring experience in detail.

Growth Practice: Read or listen to something inspiring for 10 minutes.

Day 5: Connection Deepening
Morning Practice: Choose someone you want to connect with more deeply today.

Daily Practice: Gratitude journaling + have a meaningful conversation with your chosen person.

Evening Reflection: Write about what you learned about this person.

Mindfulness Moment: Practice mindful listening during all conversations.

Day 6: Strength Recognition
Morning Practice: Identify one of your strengths and plan to use it today. *Daily Practice*:

Gratitude journaling + consciously apply your strength.

Evening Reflection: Write about how using your strength made you feel.

Self-Care Practice: Do something nurturing for your body (stretch, bath, healthy meal).

Day 7: Weekly Review
Morning Practice: Review your week and identify patterns or insights.

Daily Practice: Gratitude journaling + celebrate your consistency.

Evening Reflection: Write about the biggest change you've noticed this week.

Planning Practice: Set intentions for week two.

Week 2: Expanding Awareness (Days 8-14)
The second week builds on your foundation while introducing new practices and increasing awareness of happiness patterns.

Day 8: Optimism Practice
Morning Practice: Write down three positive things you expect from today.

Daily Practice: Gratitude journaling + look for evidence that supports your positive expectations.

Evening Reflection: Note how focusing on positive expectations affected your day.

Challenge Practice: Reframe one negative thought into a more balanced perspective.

Day 9: Flow Seeking
Morning Practice: Identify an activity that typically creates flow for you.

Daily Practice: Gratitude journaling + engage in your flow activity for at least 30 minutes.

Evening Reflection: Describe the flow experience and how it felt.

Connection Practice: Share your flow experience with someone you trust.

Day 10: Forgiveness Focus
Morning Practice: Identify someone (including yourself) you need to forgive.

Daily Practice: Gratitude journaling + write a forgiveness letter (you don't have to send it).

Evening Reflection: Notice how the forgiveness practice affected your emotional state.

Self-Care Practice: Practice self-compassion if the forgiveness work was difficult.

Day 11: Nature Connection
Morning Practice: Plan to spend time in nature today.

Daily Practice: Gratitude journaling + spend at least 20 minutes outdoors mindfully.

Evening Reflection: Write about how nature affected your mood and perspective.

Mindfulness Moment: Practice nature-based mindfulness (listening to birds, feeling wind, etc.).

Day 12: Creativity Expression
Morning Practice: Choose a creative activity to engage in today.

Daily Practice: Gratitude journaling + spend time in creative expression.

Evening Reflection: Describe how creativity made you feel and what you created.

Growth Practice: Reflect on how creativity connects to your sense of purpose.

Day 13: Service and Contribution
Morning Practice: Identify a way to serve or contribute to others today.

Daily Practice: Gratitude journaling + engage in your chosen service activity.

Evening Reflection: Write about the impact of serving others on your own well-being.

Connection Practice: Express appreciation to someone who serves you regularly.

Day 14: Week Two Review
Morning Practice: Review your progress and identify your most effective practices.

Daily Practice: Gratitude journaling + celebrate your growth.

Evening Reflection: Write about how your happiness has evolved over two weeks.

Planning Practice: Choose your three favorite practices to continue into week three.

Week 3: Deepening Practice (Days 15-21)
The third week focuses on deepening your most effective practices while addressing obstacles and building resilience.

Day 15: Obstacle Identification
Morning Practice: Identify your biggest happiness obstacles.

Daily Practice: Gratitude journaling + practice one strategy for overcoming your main bstacle.

Evening Reflection: Write about what you learned about your happiness barriers.

Challenge Practice: Use the ABCDE method to reframe a limiting belief.

Day 16: Energy Management
Morning Practice: Assess your energy levels and plan to protect them today.

Daily Practice: Gratitude journaling + practice saying no to one energy-draining activity.

Evening Reflection: Notice how protecting your energy affected your happiness.

Self-Care Practice: Engage in an activity that restores your energy.

Day 17: Value Alignment
Morning Practice: Review your core values and plan to honor them today.

Daily Practice: Gratitude journaling + make one decision based on your values.

Evening Reflection: Write about how value-aligned living affected your satisfaction.

Growth Practice: Identify one area where your life could better reflect your values.

Day 18: Relationship Investment
Morning Practice: Choose one important relationship to invest in today.

Daily Practice: Gratitude journaling + spend quality time with your chosen person.

Evening Reflection: Write about how relationship investment affected both of you.

Connection Practice: Express specific appreciation for this person's role in your life.

Day 19: Meaning Making
Morning Practice: Reflect on your life purpose and how today's activities connect to it.

Daily Practice: Gratitude journaling + engage in one purposeful activity.

Evening Reflection: Write about how connecting to purpose affected your motivation and satisfaction.

Growth Practice: Identify one way to increase meaning in your daily life.

Day 20: Resilience Building
Morning Practice: Recall a time when you overcame adversity and identify the strengths you used.

Daily Practice: Gratitude journaling + practice one resilience-building activity.

Evening Reflection: Write about how focusing on resilience affected your confidence.

Challenge Practice: Identify one current challenge and brainstorm three possible responses.

Day 21: Week Three Review
Morning Practice: Assess your progress and identify your strongest happiness habits.

Daily Practice: Gratitude journaling + celebrate your commitment and growth.

Evening Reflection: Write about the most significant changes you've noticed.

Planning Practice: Design your ideal daily happiness routine for the final week.

Week 4: Integration and Sustainability (Days 22-30)
The final week focuses on integrating your learning into a sustainable long-term practice and planning for continued growth.

Day 22: Habit Integration
Morning Practice: Review all practices and choose your top 5 for long-term use.

Daily Practice: Implement your chosen practices in a streamlined routine.

Evening Reflection: Evaluate how well your integrated routine worked.

Planning Practice: Adjust your routine based on what felt most natural and effective.

Day 23: Sharing Your Journey
Morning Practice: Identify someone who would benefit from hearing about your happiness journey.

Daily Practice: Continue your integrated routine + share your experience with your chosen person.

Evening Reflection: Write about how sharing your journey affected both you and the other person.

Connection Practice: Invite someone to join you in practicing happiness habits.

Day 24: Future Visioning
Morning Practice: Visualize yourself one year from now, having maintained your happiness practices.

Daily Practice: Continue your integrated routine + take one action toward your vision.

Evening Reflection: Write about your vision and how it motivates you.

Growth Practice: Set three specific happiness goals for the next three months.

Day 25: Challenge Preparation
Morning Practice: Anticipate future obstacles to your happiness practice.

Daily Practice: Continue your integrated routine + create strategies for overcoming anticipated challenges.

Evening Reflection: Write about your obstacle-prevention strategies.

Planning Practice: Create a "happiness emergency kit" for difficult days.

Day 26: Community Building
Morning Practice: Identify ways to build a supportive community around your happiness journey.

Daily Practice: Continue your integrated routine + take one step toward building your happiness community.

Evening Reflection: Write about the importance of community support for sustained well-being.

Connection Practice: Reach out to someone who shares your commitment to personal growth.

Day 27: Gratitude Celebration
Morning Practice: Write a comprehensive gratitude letter to yourself, acknowledging your commitment and growth.

Daily Practice: Continue your integrated routine + practice extra gratitude throughout the day.

Evening Reflection: Read your self-gratitude letter and write about how it feels to acknowledge your progress.

Celebration Practice: Do something special to celebrate your dedication to happiness.

Day 28: Wisdom Integration
Morning Practice: Review your journal entries and identify the most important insights from your journey.

Daily Practice: Continue your integrated routine + write a letter of advice to someone starting their happiness journey.

Evening Reflection: Write about the wisdom you've gained and how you want to apply it.

Growth Practice: Identify your next area of personal development focus.

Day 29: Commitment Renewal
Morning Practice: Reflect on your "why" for pursuing happiness and renew your commitment.

Daily Practice: Continue your integrated routine + make a formal commitment to your ongoing happiness practice.

Evening Reflection: Write about your renewed commitment and what it means to you.

Planning Practice: Schedule regular check-ins with yourself to maintain accountability.

Day 30: Celebration and New Beginning
Morning Practice: Complete your final happiness assessment to measure your progress.

Daily Practice: Continue your integrated routine + celebrate your 30-day achievement.

Evening Reflection: Write a comprehensive reflection on your entire journey.

Future Practice: Set intentions for your ongoing happiness journey beyond the challenge.

Daily Tracking and Progress Measurement

Throughout the challenge, track your progress using these simple metrics:
- **Daily Mood Rating**: Rate your overall mood each evening on a scale of 1-10.
- **Energy Level**: Assess your energy level each evening on a scale of 1-10.
- **Practice Completion**: Check off which practices you completed each day.
- **Insight Capture**: Write one key insight or observation each day.
- **Gratitude Count**: Note how many things you felt grateful for beyond your formal practice.
- **Connection Quality**: Rate the quality of your social interactions each day.
- **Stress Level**: Assess your stress level each evening on a scale of 1-10.

Celebrating Wins and Maintaining Momentum

Weekly Celebrations.

At the end of each week, celebrate your consistency and progress:
- Acknowledge your commitment to showing up daily
- Review your most meaningful insights
- Notice positive changes in your mood, relationships, or perspective
- Share your progress with a supportive friend or family member
- Do something special to honor your dedication

Progress Indicators to Watch For
- Increased awareness of positive moments throughout your day
- Greater resilience when facing challenges
- Improved relationships and social connections
- Enhanced sense of purpose and meaning
- Better physical energy and sleep quality
- Reduced anxiety and worry
- Increased optimism about the future
- Greater self-compassion and acceptance

Reflection: What Changed After 30 Days?

At the completion of your challenge, engage in comprehensive reflection:

Quantitative Changes
- Compare your initial and final happiness assessments
- Review your daily mood and energy ratings for trends
- Calculate your practice completion percentage

- Identify which practices you found most and least helpful

Qualitative Changes
- How has your perspective on happiness evolved?
- What surprised you most about the journey?
- Which relationships have been positively affected?
- How do you handle stress and challenges differently?
- What aspects of your life feel more meaningful?
- How has your self-talk and inner dialogue changed?

Integration Planning
- Which practices will you continue long-term?
- How will you maintain accountability for your happiness habits?
- What support systems will help you sustain your progress?
- How will you handle setbacks or difficult periods?
- What's your next area of focus for personal growth?

Action: Share Your Happiness Journey with Others

The final action of your challenge is to share your experience with others, creating ripple effects of positive change:

Step 1: Document Your Story
Write a brief summary of your 30-day journey, including:
- Your motivation for starting the challenge
- Your biggest insights and changes
- The practices that worked best for you
- Advice for others considering the journey

Step 2: Choose Your Sharing Method
Select ways to share that feel authentic to you:
- Social media posts about your experience
- Conversations with friends and family
- Presentation to colleagues or community groups
- Blog post or article about your journey
- Mentoring someone who wants to start their own challenge

Step 3: Create Ongoing Accountability
Establish systems to maintain your progress:
- Find an accountability partner for continued practice
- Join or create a happiness practice group

- Schedule regular check-ins with yourself
- Plan periodic "happiness retreats" or intensive practice periods

Step 4: Pay It Forward

Look for opportunities to support others' happiness journeys:

- Offer to guide someone through the 30-day challenge
- Share resources and tools that helped you
- Model happiness practices in your daily interactions
- Create positive environments in your family, workplace, or community

Remember, completing the 30-day challenge is not the end of your happiness journey—it's the beginning of a lifetime practice of intentional well-being. The habits and insights you've developed will continue to compound, creating ever-greater levels of fulfillment and positive impact on others.

Appendices & Resources

Appendix A: Happiness Self-Assessment Worksheet

This comprehensive assessment helps you understand your current happiness landscape and track progress over time.

Life Satisfaction Assessment

Rate each area from 1 (very dissatisfied) to 10 (very satisfied):

Life Area	Initial Rating	30-Day Rating	90-Day Rating	Notes
Career and Work	___	___	___	
Relationships and Social Connections	___	___	___	
Physical Health and Energy	___	___	___	
Financial Security	___	___	___	
Personal Growth and Learning	___	___	___	
Recreation and Fun	___	___	___	
Contribution and Service	___	___	___	
Spiritual/Philosophical Well-being	___	___	___	
Overall Life Satisfaction	___	___	___	

PERMA Assessment

Rate each element from 1 (very low) to 10 (very high):

PERMA Element	Initial	30-Day	90-Day	Specific Examples
Positive Emotions - Joy, gratitude, serenity, hope	___	___	___	
Engagement - Flow experiences, using strengths	___	___	___	
Relationships - Quality connections, social support	___	___	___	

Meaning - Purpose, values alignment, contribution	—	—	—	
Accomplishment - Achievement, mastery, progress	—	—	—	

Happiness Habits Frequency

Rate how often you engage in each practice: Daily (4), Weekly (3), Monthly (2), Rarely (1), Never (0)

Practice	Initial	30-Day	90-Day	Notes
Expressing gratitude	—	—	—	
Physical exercise	—	—	—	
Mindfulness/meditation	—	—	—	
Quality time with loved ones	—	—	—	
Pursuing meaningful goals	—	—	—	
Acts of kindness	—	—	—	
Engaging in flow activities	—	—	—	
Adequate sleep (7-9 hours)	—	—	—	
Time in nature	—	—	—	
Creative expression	—	—	—	

Happiness Obstacles Identification

Check all that apply and rate their impact (1 = minor, 5 = major):

- [ ] Negative self-talk and inner criticism ___
- [ ] Toxic or draining relationships ___
- [ ] Overwhelming stress or busyness ___
- [ ] Lack of purpose or direction ___
- [ ] Poor physical health habits ___
- [ ] Financial worries ___
- [ ] Comparison with others ___
- [ ] Perfectionism ___

- [ ] Past trauma or unresolved grief ___
- [ ] Social isolation or loneliness ___
- [ ] Work dissatisfaction ___
- [ ] Lack of personal time ___

Values and Purpose Clarity
1. **Core Values Identification**: List your top 5 values in order of importance:
2. **Values Alignment**: Rate how well your current life aligns with each core value (1-10): Value 1: ___ Value 2: ___ Value 3: ___ Value 4: ___ Value 5: ___
3. **Purpose Statement**: Write a brief statement of your life purpose:
4. **Meaning Sources**: What gives your life the most meaning?

Appendix B: Gratitude and Savoring Journal Templates

Daily Gratitude Journal Template
Date: _____

Three Things I'm Grateful For Today:

1. **What:** _____
   Why: _____
   How it made me feel: _____
2. **What:** _____
   Why: _____
   How it made me feel: _____
3. **What:** _____
   Why: _____
   How it made me feel: _____

Gratitude Letter to Someone Special:
Dear _____,

I want to express my heartfelt gratitude for…

___

Weekly Gratitude Reflection:
- What patterns do I notice in what I'm grateful for?
- How has practicing gratitude affected my mood this week?
- What am I taking for granted that I could appreciate more?

Savoring Practice Template
Date: _____

Experience I Want to Savor Today:

Before the Experience (Anticipation):
- How am I looking forward to this?
- What do I hope to notice or feel?

During the Experience (Present-Moment Savoring):
- What do I see, hear, smell, taste, or feel?
- What emotions am I experiencing?
- How can I slow down and fully absorb this moment?

After the Experience (Reminiscence):
- What was the best part of this experience?
- How did savoring enhance my enjoyment?
- What details do I want to remember?

Weekly Savoring Reflection:
- Which experiences brought me the most joy this week?
- How did intentional savoring change my experience?
- What simple pleasures did I discover or rediscover?

Appendix C: Affirmation and Mindset Reframing Scripts

Daily Affirmations for Happiness
Morning Affirmations (Choose 3-5 that resonate with you):
- "I choose to focus on what brings me joy and fulfillment today"
- "I am worthy of happiness and all good things in life"
- "I have the power to create positive experiences through my choices"
- "I am grateful for this new day and the opportunities it brings"
- "I treat myself and others with kindness and compassion"
- "I am growing stronger and wiser through every experience"
- "I attract positive people and experiences into my life"
- "I find meaning and purpose in both ordinary and extraordinary moments"

Evening Affirmations:
- "I acknowledge my efforts and progress today"
- "I release any negativity from today and embrace peace"
- "I am proud of how I showed up today"

- "I trust that tomorrow brings new possibilities"

Mindset Reframing Scripts

For Perfectionism:
- Old thought: "I must do this perfectly or I'm a failure"
- New thought: "I will do my best and learn from the experience"
- Reframing script: "Progress, not perfection, is my goal. Every effort teaches me something valuable."

For Comparison:
- Old thought: "Everyone else has it better than me"
- New thought: "Everyone has their own journey with unique challenges and blessings"
- Reframing script: "I celebrate others' success while focusing on my own growth and gratitude for what I have."

For Catastrophizing:
- Old thought: "This will be a disaster"
- New thought: "I can handle whatever happens, and there are multiple possible outcomes"
- Reframing script: "I prepare for challenges while remaining open to positive possibilities."

For Self-Criticism:
- Old thought: "I'm not good enough"
- New thought: "I am learning and growing, and I have many valuable qualities"
- Reframing script: "I speak to myself with the same kindness I would show a good friend."

Self-Compassion Scripts

For Difficult Moments:

"This is a moment of suffering. Suffering is part of the human experience. May I be kind to myself right now. May I give myself the compassion I need."

For Mistakes:

"I am human, and humans make mistakes. This mistake doesn't define me. I can learn from this and do better next time. I forgive myself and choose to move forward with wisdom."

For Setbacks:

"Setbacks are temporary and don't determine my future. I have overcome challenges before, and I can do it again. I am resilient and capable of growth."

Appendix D: 30-Day Happiness Challenge Tracker

Week 1: Foundation Building

Day	Gratitude Journal	Mindfulness Practice	Kindness Act	Self-Care	Mood (1-10)	Energy (1-10)	Notes
1	☐	☐	☐	☐	___	___	
2	☐	☐	☐	☐	___	___	
3	☐	☐	☐	☐	___	___	
4	☐	☐	☐	☐	___	___	
5	☐	☐	☐	☐	___	___	
6	☐	☐	☐	☐	___	___	
7	☐	☐	☐	☐	___	___	

Week 2: Expanding Awareness

Day	Gratitude Journal	Daily Focus	Connection Practice	Growth Activity	Mood (1-10)	Energy (1-10)	Key Insight
8	☐	Optimism	☐	☐	___	___	
9	☐	Flow	☐	☐	___	___	
10	☐	Forgiveness	☐	☐	___	___	
11	☐	Nature	☐	☐	___	___	
12	☐	Creativity	☐	☐	___	___	
13	☐	Service	☐	☐	___	___	
14	☐	Review	☐	☐	___	___	

Week 3: Deepening Practice

Day	Core Practices	Challenge Focus	Reflection Quality	Mood (1-10)	Energy (1-10)	Breakthrough Moment
15	☐	Obstacles	☐	___	___	
16	☐	Energy	☐	___	___	

17	☐	Values	☐	___	___	
18	☐	Relationships	☐	___	___	
19	☐	Meaning	☐	___	___	
20	☐	Resilience	☐	___	___	
21	☐	Integration	☐	___	___	

Week 4: Integration and Sustainability

Day	Integrated Routine	Sharing/Community	Future Planning	Mood (1-10)	Energy (1-10)	Commitment Level
22	☐	☐	☐	___	___	
23	☐	☐	☐	___	___	
24	☐	☐	☐	___	___	
25	☐	☐	☐	___	___	
26	☐	☐	☐	___	___	
27	☐	☐	☐	___	___	
28	☐	☐	☐	___	___	
29	☐	☐	☐	___	___	
30	☐	☐	☐	___	___	

30-Day Summary
- Total days completed: ___/30
- Average mood rating: ___
- Average energy rating: ___
- Most effective practices: _____
- Biggest challenges: _____
- Most significant changes: _____
- Practices to continue: _____

Appendix E: Recommended Books, Podcasts, and Apps

Essential Books on Happiness and Well-Being
Foundational Texts:
- *Authentic Happiness* by Martin Seligman - The foundational text of positive psychology
- *The How of Happiness* by Sonja Lyubomirsky - Science-based strategies for increasing well-being
- *Flourish* by Martin Seligman - The PERMA model and well-being theory
- *The Happiness Hypothesis* by Jonathan Haidt - Ancient wisdom meets modern science

Practical Applications:
- *The Happiness Project* by Gretchen Rubin - A year-long happiness experiment
- *10% Happier* by Dan Harris - Meditation and mindfulness for skeptics
- *The Gifts of Imperfection* by Brené Brown - Courage, compassion, and connection
- *Atomic Habits* by James Clear - Building habits that support well-being

Deeper Exploration:
- *Man's Search for Meaning* by Viktor Frankl - Finding purpose through adversity
- *The Power of Now* by Eckhart Tolle - Present-moment awareness
- *Mindset* by Carol Dweck - Growth mindset and resilience
- *The Upward Spiral* by Alex Korb - Neuroscience of depression and happiness

Helpful Podcasts
Happiness and Well-Being Focused:
- *The Happiness Lab* with Dr. Laurie Santos - Science-based happiness strategies
- *Ten Percent Happier* with Dan Harris - Meditation and mindfulness discussions
- *The Life Coach School Podcast* with Brooke Castillo - Thought work and emotional management
- *Happier with Gretchen Rubin* - Practical happiness tips and habits

Personal Development:
- *The Tim Ferriss Show* - Interviews with high performers on habits and practices
- *On Purpose* with Jay Shetty - Meaning, purpose, and intentional living
- *The School of Greatness* with Lewis Howes - Personal growth and achievement
- *Unlocking Us* with Brené Brown - Vulnerability, courage, and connection

Recommended Apps

Meditation and Mindfulness:
- *Headspace* - Guided meditations and mindfulness exercises
- *Calm* - Meditation, sleep stories, and relaxation tools
- *Insight Timer* - Free meditations and timer with community features
- *Ten Percent Happier* - Practical meditation courses

Gratitude and Journaling:
- *Five Minute Journal* - Structured gratitude and reflection prompts
- *Gratitude* - Simple gratitude journaling with photo integration
- *Day One* - Comprehensive journaling with multimedia support
- *Reflectly* - AI-powered journaling for emotional awareness

Habit Tracking:
- *Habitica* - Gamified habit tracking and goal achievement
- *Streaks* - Simple, visual habit tracking
- *Way of Life* - Color-coded habit and activity tracking
- *Productive* - Beautiful, intuitive habit tracker

Well-Being and Mood:
- *Sanvello* - Mood tracking, anxiety management, and coping tools
- *Happify* - Science-based activities and games for happiness
- *Youper* - AI emotional health assistant
- *MindShift* - Anxiety management and cognitive behavioral therapy tools

Appendix F: Further Reading and Support Communities

Academic Resources

Research Journals:
- *Journal of Positive Psychology* - Latest research in positive psychology
- *Applied Psychology: Health and Well-Being* - Practical applications of well-being research
- *Journal of Happiness Studies* - Interdisciplinary happiness research
- *Emotion* - Research on emotional processes and regulation

Research Centers:
- *Penn Positive Psychology Center* (University of Pennsylvania) - Martin Seligman's research hub
- *Greater Good Science Center* (UC Berkeley) - Science of meaningful life

- Stanford Center for Compassion and Altruism - Research on compassion and well-being
- Yale Center for Emotional Intelligence - Emotional skills and well-being

Online Learning Platforms

Free Courses:

- *The Science of Well-Being* (Yale/Coursera) - Comprehensive happiness course
- *Positive Psychology* (Penn/Coursera) - Introduction to positive psychology
- Mindfulness for Wellbeing and Peak Performance (Monash/FutureLearn)
- Positive Psychology and Mental Health (EdX/University of Texas)

Paid Platforms:

- *The Great Courses* - In-depth lectures on psychology and well-being
- *MasterClass* - Courses on mindfulness, resilience, and personal development
- *Mindvalley* - Personal growth and consciousness courses
- *The Shift Network* - Transformational learning programs

Support Communities

Online Communities:

- *Reddit r/getmotivated* - Motivation and inspiration community
- *Reddit r/decidingtobebetter* - Personal improvement discussions
- *Facebook Groups* - Search for "happiness," "positive psychology," or "personal growth"
- *Meetup Groups* - Local happiness and personal development meetups

Professional Support:

- *Psychology Today* - Directory of therapists specializing in positive psychology
- International Positive Psychology Association (IPPA) - Professional network and resources
- *Action for Happiness* - Global movement for happier communities
- *The Flourishing Institute* - Positive psychology coaching and training

Creating Your Own Support Network:

Family and Friends:

- Share your happiness journey with loved ones
- Invite others to join you in happiness practices
- Create family or friend challenges around well-being
- Establish regular check-ins about personal growth

Workplace Communities:
- Start a workplace happiness or wellness group
- Organize lunch-and-learn sessions on well-being topics
- Create peer support partnerships for personal development
- Advocate for workplace well-being initiatives

Local Communities:
- Join or start a book club focused on personal development
- Participate in community service organizations
- Attend local workshops or seminars on happiness and well-being
- Create neighborhood walking groups or outdoor activity clubs

Final Reflection & Series Roadmap

As you complete your journey through "Happiness That Matters," you've not only learned about the science and practice of well-being—you've experienced firsthand how intentional choices can transform your daily experience of life. This final section helps you integrate your learning with the broader "About Things That Matter" series and plan your continued growth.

Key Questions for Ongoing Happiness and Fulfillment

Your happiness journey doesn't end with this book—it evolves and deepens throughout your life. These questions will guide your ongoing reflection and growth:

Daily Reflection Questions:
- What am I grateful for today, and why?
- How did I contribute to someone else's well-being today?
- What moments did I fully savor and appreciate?
- How did I honor my values in my choices today?
- What challenged me today, and how did I respond?

Weekly Reflection Questions:
- Which happiness practices served me best this week?
- How did my emotional state affect my relationships and productivity?
- What patterns do I notice in my mood and energy levels?
- Where did I experience flow and deep engagement?
- How did I grow or learn something new about myself?

Monthly Reflection Questions:
- How has my understanding of happiness evolved?
- What obstacles to my well-being have I overcome or need to address?
- How well is my life aligned with my core values and purpose?
- What relationships need more attention and investment?
- What new practices or experiences do I want to explore?

Annual Reflection Questions:
- How have I grown as a person over the past year?
- What contributions have I made to others' happiness and well-being?
- How have my priorities and values shifted or deepened?
- What legacy am I creating through my daily choices?

- What does happiness mean to me now compared to a year ago?

How Happiness Amplifies Change, Goals, Time, and Relationships

Happiness is not separate from the other areas covered in the "About Things That Matter" series—it's the foundation that makes everything else more effective and fulfilling.

Happiness and Change

When you're genuinely happy, change becomes easier and more natural:

- **Increased Resilience**: Happy people bounce back faster from setbacks and view challenges as opportunities for growth
- **Enhanced Creativity**: Positive emotions broaden your thinking, helping you find innovative solutions to problems
- **Greater Motivation**: When you feel good, you have more energy to invest in personal transformation
- **Reduced Resistance**: Happiness reduces the fear and anxiety that often accompany change
- **Sustainable Progress**: Joy in the journey makes long-term change more sustainable than willpower alone

Happiness and Goals

Your well-being transforms how you approach and achieve your aspirations:

- **Clearer Vision**: Happy people are better at identifying what truly matters to them
- **Intrinsic Motivation**: You're more likely to pursue goals that align with your values rather than external expectations
- **Process Enjoyment**: Finding satisfaction in the journey makes goal pursuit more fulfilling
- **Balanced Achievement**: Happiness helps you pursue success without sacrificing relationships or health
- **Meaningful Accomplishment**: Your achievements feel more satisfying when they emerge from a foundation of well-being

Happiness and Time

Well-being completely changes your relationship with time:

- **Present-Moment Awareness**: Happy people are more likely to be fully present rather than anxious about the future or regretful about the past
- **Prioritization Clarity**: When you know what brings you joy and meaning, time management becomes more intuitive

- **Energy Management**: Happiness provides sustainable energy for your most important activities
- **Savoring Ability**: You naturally slow down to appreciate positive experiences
- **Patience Development**: Contentment reduces the urgency that leads to poor time choices

Happiness and Relationships

Perhaps nowhere is the impact of happiness more evident than in your connections with others:

- **Emotional Contagion**: Your positive emotions literally improve others' well-being
- **Increased Empathy**: Happy people are more attuned to others' needs and emotions
- **Better Communication**: Positive emotions enhance your ability to listen, understand, and express yourself
- **Conflict Resolution**: Happiness provides the emotional stability needed for constructive problem-solving
- **Deeper Intimacy**: When you're comfortable with yourself, you can be more vulnerable and authentic with others

Integration Practices for the Complete Series

To maximize the synergy between happiness and the other "Things That Matter" areas:

Weekly Integration Review:

- **Monday**: Set happiness intentions for the week while planning your goals and schedule
- **Wednesday**: Check in on how your emotional state is affecting your productivity and relationships
- **Friday**: Reflect on how pursuing your goals and managing your time supported or hindered your well-being
- **Sunday**: Plan how to better integrate happiness practices with your other priorities

Monthly Cross-Series Assessment:

- Rate your satisfaction in each area: Change, Goals, Time, Relationships, and Happiness
- Identify connections between your ratings—how does progress in one area affect others?
- Choose one integration practice to focus on for the coming month
- Celebrate the compound benefits of working on multiple areas simultaneously

Quarterly Life Design Sessions:

- Review your progress across all five areas

- Identify your biggest insights about how these areas interact
- Adjust your practices and priorities based on what you've learned
- Set intentions for deeper integration in the coming quarter

Invitation to the About Things That Matter Community

Your journey through this series connects you to a global community of people committed to intentional, meaningful living. We invite you to:

Share Your Story:

- Document your transformation and insights from implementing these practices
- Share your experiences on social media using #ThingsThatMatter
- Write reviews and recommendations to help others discover these resources
- Create content (blogs, videos, podcasts) about your journey

Connect with Others:

- Join our online community at [website/platform]
- Attend virtual or in-person meetups and workshops
- Find accountability partners who share your commitment to growth
- Participate in group challenges and learning experiences

Contribute to the Movement:

- Mentor others who are beginning their journey
- Lead book clubs or study groups in your community
- Advocate for well-being initiatives in your workplace or community
- Support research and organizations promoting human flourishing

Continue Learning:

- Access additional resources, tools, and updates
- Participate in advanced workshops and masterclasses
- Receive ongoing support and guidance for your practices
- Stay informed about new research and developments in these areas

Your Ongoing Happiness Journey

As you close this book and continue your happiness journey, remember these essential truths:

Happiness is a Practice, Not a Destination. True well-being comes from daily choices and habits, not from achieving specific circumstances or goals. Your happiness practice will evolve and deepen throughout your life.

Small Steps Create Big Changes. The Kaizen approach applies to all areas of life. Tiny, consistent improvements in your happiness practices will compound into significant transformation over time.

Your Happiness Matters to Others. By cultivating your own well-being, you create ripple effects that positively impact everyone around you. Your happiness is a gift to the world.

Integration Amplifies Impact. The synergy between happiness, change, goals, time, and relationships creates exponential benefits. Working on these areas together is more powerful than addressing them separately.

Community Accelerates Growth. Surrounding yourself with others who share your commitment to intentional living will support and accelerate your progress while making the journey more enjoyable.

You Have Everything You Need. Within you right now are all the resources necessary for genuine happiness and fulfillment. These books and practices simply help you access and develop what's already there.

Final Commitment

As you complete "Happiness That Matters," make this commitment to yourself:

"I commit to treating my happiness not as a luxury but as a responsibility—to myself and to everyone whose life I touch. I will practice the habits and mindset that create genuine well-being, knowing that my joy contributes to a happier, more compassionate world. I will be patient with myself as I grow, celebrate my progress along the way, and remember that happiness is both a journey and a destination—found not in some distant future, but in how I choose to live today."

Your signature: _____ Date: _____

Welcome to a lifetime of happiness that truly matters—not just for you, but for everyone whose life you touch. The world needs your unique contribution, and that contribution is most powerful when it flows from a foundation of genuine well-being and joy.

The journey continues...

Bibliography

Foundational Books and Leading Authors

Martin Seligman

- *Authentic Happiness* — foundational text of positive psychology
- *Flourish* — well-being theory and the PERMA model

Sonja Lyubomirsky

- *The How of Happiness* — science-based strategies for increasing well-being

Jonathan Haidt

- *The Happiness Hypothesis* — ancient wisdom meets modern science

Viktor Frankl

- *Man's Search for Meaning* — purpose through adversity

James Clear

- *Atomic Habits* — building habits that support well-being

Gretchen Rubin

- *The Happiness Project* — a year-long happiness experiment

Dan Harris

- *10% Happier* — meditation and mindfulness for skeptics

Brené Brown

- *The Gifts of Imperfection* and *Unlocking Us* (podcast) — courage, compassion, and connection

Jay Shetty

- *On Purpose* (book and podcast) — intentional living and meaning

Eckhart Tolle

- *The Power of Now* — present-moment awareness

Carol Dweck

- *Mindset* — growth mindset and resilience

Alex Korb

- *The Upward Spiral* — neuroscience of depression and happiness

Key Research Studies and Academic References

- **The Harvard Grant Study** — 80-year longitudinal study on human flourishing
- **The Framingham Heart Study (Social Networks)** — how happiness spreads through social networks

Research journals and centers:

- Journal of Positive Psychology
- Applied Psychology: Health and Well-Being
- Journal of Happiness Studies
- Emotion
- Penn Positive Psychology Center (University of Pennsylvania)
- Greater Good Science Center (UC Berkeley)
- Stanford Center for Compassion and Altruism
- Yale Center for Emotional Intelligence

Kaizen Principle — continuous improvement, as drawn from Japanese methodology and applied in the 30-Day Happiness Challenge

Recommended Podcasts and Apps

- *The Happiness Lab* (Dr. Laurie Santos)
- Ten Percent Happier (Dan Harris)
- *Happier* (Gretchen Rubin)
- *On Purpose* (Jay Shetty)
- Meditation: Headspace, Calm, Insight Timer, Ten Percent Happier
- Journaling: Five Minute Journal, Gratitude, Day One, Reflectly
- Habit Trackers: Habitica, Streaks, Way of Life, Productive

Notable Influences and Concepts

- **PERMA Model** (Positive Emotions, Engagement, Relationships, Meaning, Accomplishment) by Martin Seligman
- Habit science from MIT, Stanford research on mindset, organizational psychology literature, and various studies from clinical and academic fields on meaning and well-being.

PART 3 – THE 24-HOUR MIRACLE THAT MATTERS

To everyone who wants to spend more time on what truly matters, and less on what doesn't.

"We shall never have more time. We have, and have always had, all the time there is."—**Arnold Bennett**

"The chief beauty about time is that you cannot waste it in advance. The next year, the next day, the next hour are lying ready for you."—**Arnold Bennett**

"It is not that we have a short space of time, but that we waste much of it. Life is long enough, and it has been given in sufficiently generous measure to allow the accomplishment of the very greatest things if the whole of it is well invested."— **Lucius Annaeus Seneca**

The 24-Hour Miracle That Matters
TIME MANAGEMENT HABITS OF SUCCESSFUL PEOPLE

About Things That Matter
A SELF-IMPROVEMENT SERIES FOR SUCCESS

Book 7

JC Ryan

About This Book

"The 24-Hour Miracle That Matters" by JC Ryan is a modern guide to time management that champions a compassionate and realistic approach to personal change. Drawing inspiration from timeless thinkers like Arnold Bennett and Seneca, the book emphasizes that while the quantity of time remains eternally fixed at 1,440 minutes per day, the pressures of our contemporary world have changed how we use it. Instead of advocating for strict, perfectionist productivity, Ryan encourages a flexible, forgiving framework centered on self-compassion.

A key message is that meaningful change requires honest trade-offs, urging readers to recognize what they're willing to sacrifice for positive transformation. The book acknowledges daily imperfections and inevitable failures, advocating for "gentle encouragement" and persistence rather than judgment. Practical exercises—such as putting on workout clothes without committing to exercise and tracking only completion—reflect this philosophy, focusing on building habits through achievable steps.

Ryan critiques the cycle of reactive modern living: rushing through mornings, spending energy at work, and defaulting to passive, forgettable leisure in the evenings. He challenges readers to invest their limited daily minutes purposefully, finding depth and meaning in ordinary routines. Ultimately, the book is both a realistic antidote to toxic productivity and a manual for discovering the extraordinary in everyday life.

Preface

In 1908, Arnold Bennett published a slim volume that would become one of the most enduring works on time and life management ever written. *How to Live on 24 Hours a Day* spoke to Edwardian clerks who felt trapped by their routines, offering them a radical proposition: that their "real" life didn't begin after work, but was happening every moment of every day. Bennett's message was revolutionary for its time—and it may be even more vital for ours.

Today, more than a century later, we face a paradox Bennett could never have imagined. We live in an age of unprecedented convenience, where technology promises to save us time at every turn. We can communicate instantly across continents, summon transportation with a tap, and access the world's knowledge from devices in our pockets. Yet somehow, we feel more time-starved than ever. The very tools designed to free us have become digital leashes, tethering us to an endless stream of notifications, updates, and demands for our attention.

Where Bennett's readers struggled with the monotony of routine, we struggle with the tyranny of choice. Where they faced boredom, we face overwhelm. Where they had too little stimulation, we have far too much. The modern world doesn't just steal our time—it fragments it into ever-smaller pieces, leaving us feeling scattered, anxious, and perpetually behind.

This is why *The 24-Hour Miracle That Matters* is not merely an update of Bennett's classic, but an urgent manual for our times. While honoring Bennett's core insight—that we all have the same 24 hours and the power to transform how we use them—this modern edition addresses the unique challenges of living in a hyper-connected, always-on world. It speaks to those who check their phones before their feet hit the floor, who eat lunch at their desks while answering emails, who fall asleep scrolling through the curated lives of strangers.

The principles Bennett outlined remain timeless: the importance of intentional living, the value of mental cultivation, the need to claim ownership of our hours. But the application of these principles requires new strategies for new struggles. How do we find focus in an economy built on distraction? How do we create boundaries when work follows us home in our pockets? How do we cultivate depth when algorithms reward us for skimming surfaces?

This book offers answers—not perfect solutions, but practical wisdom for imperfect people trying to live meaningful lives in demanding times. It acknowledges that the path to intentional living is harder now than it was in Bennett's day, but also that it's more necessary. In a world designed to scatter our attention and monetize our distraction, the ability to direct our own hours becomes an act of quiet rebellion.

Perhaps most importantly, this modern edition embraces something Bennett, writing in a more formal age, could only hint at: the need for self-compassion in our efforts to change. It recognizes that we will fail, that we will be imperfect, that some days the best we can do is simply show up. It offers not a rigid system but a flexible framework, not harsh discipline but gentle encouragement, not judgment but understanding.

As you read these pages, you'll find Bennett's wisdom translated for our times—infused with humor, grounded in modern research, and tempered with the recognition that life is messy and change is hard. You'll discover that the goal isn't to optimize every moment or transform into a productivity machine, but to live with greater intention, presence, and joy within the constraints and challenges of modern life.

The 24-hour miracle hasn't changed since Bennett's time. Each day, you still receive the same generous gift: 1,440 minutes to use as you choose. What has changed is the world in which we must use them. This book is your guide to navigating that world—to finding pockets of peace in the chaos, moments of depth in the shallows, and the extraordinary within your ordinary days.

Your time is your life. This book will help you reclaim both.

Prologue: The Midnight Realization

It's 2:47 AM, and you're awake. Again.

Not because of insomnia or a crying baby or the neighbor's party. You're awake because somewhere between scrolling through your phone and mentally rehearsing tomorrow's to-do list, a thought struck you like lightning in the darkness:

Is this it?

You lie there, staring at the ceiling (or more likely, at your phone screen's blue glow), and the question expands, filling the room like fog: Is this what I'm doing with my life? This endless cycle of wake, work, scroll, sleep, repeat? These days that blur together like watercolors in rain? This constant feeling of being busy but never quite... fulfilled?

You think about your day, really think about it. The morning you can barely remember because you were already mentally at work. The afternoon that vanished into meetings and emails and tasks that seemed urgent but now, at 2:47 AM, feel utterly forgettable. The evening you meant to use productively but somehow lost to a combination of exhaustion, Netflix, and that peculiar modern talent of simultaneously watching TV while scrolling through your phone while somehow absorbing neither.

Where did the day go? Where do any of your days go?

You make a mental calculation: If you live to 80; you have roughly 29,200 days. You've already spent...how many? And how many of those do you actually remember? How many felt truly lived rather than merely survived?

The ceiling offers no answers.

You could check your phone again. See what's happening in the world, in other people's lives, in the endless stream of content designed to fill moments exactly like this one. But something stops you. Because in this quiet hour, in this pause between today and tomorrow, you've stumbled upon a truth both terrifying and liberating:

You can't buy more time. You can't save it, stretch it, or store it for later. But you can change how you live within it.

This book is for everyone who has had their own 2:47 AM moment. For those who sense that life is slipping by like sand through fingers, but don't know how to close their grip without crushing what they're trying to hold. For those who are tired of being busy but not present, productive but not purposeful, connected but not truly alive.

It's for those who have tried the life hacks and productivity systems, downloaded the apps and bought the planners, but still feel like they're missing something essential. Those who suspect that the answer isn't about doing more, but about being more—more present, more intentional, more awake to the miracle of existence, even on a random Tuesday.

You're not looking for another system to master or another routine to fail at. You're looking for a way to transform your relationship with time itself. To stop feeling like its victim and start feeling like its partner. To realize that every ordinary day holds extraordinary potential—not for superhuman achievement, but for authentic living.

The clock reads 2:52 AM now. In eight minutes, you've already begun to change. Not because of any grand resolution or life-altering decision, but because of a simple shift in awareness. You've noticed. You've questioned. You've admitted that something needs to change.

That's where all transformation begins—not with answers, but with better questions. Not with certainty, but with curiosity. Not with perfection, but with the gentle courage to try.

Tomorrow, no, today, you'll receive another gift: 24 fresh hours, delivered with the sunrise. They'll arrive like they always do, without fanfare or instruction manual. But this time, something will be different.

This time, you'll be ready.

This time, you'll know they're a miracle.

And this time, just maybe, you'll learn how to live them.

1. The Gift of 24 Hours

"Time is what we want most, but what we use worst." —**William Penn**

Every morning, without fail, you are given a gift: 24 hours. It arrives quietly, without ceremony, and expects nothing in return except that you use it. This daily allotment is the great equalizer, no one gets more, no one gets less. Whether you're a CEO, a student, a parent, or someone still figuring things out, your account is credited with the same 1,440 minutes as everyone else. Even Jeff Bezos can't Prime himself an extra hour.

Yet, despite its value, time is the resource we most often neglect. We plan our finances down to the penny, worry about our diets with religious fervor, and fret over our careers like anxious parents at a school play, but rarely do we pause to consider how we're spending the hours that make up our days. Time has a strict no-return policy, unlike money, it can't be saved for later or borrowed from tomorrow. Once it's spent, it's gone. There are no refunds, no exchanges, no store credit for unused minutes.

"The bad news is time flies. The good news is you're the pilot." —**Michael Altshuler**

It's easy to fall into the habit of treating time as an afterthought—like that gym membership you keep meaning to use. We fill our days with obligations, distractions, and routines, assuming that more time will magically appear when we need it most, perhaps delivered by some temporal fairy godmother. But the truth is, you will never have more time than you do right now. Each day is a blank slate, a fresh opportunity to choose how you want to live. Or, if you prefer, another chance to spend three hours watching cat videos.

The challenge is not to find more hours in the day (unless you've discovered time travel, in which case, please share), but to make the hours you have truly matter. This doesn't mean cramming every moment with activity or striving for relentless productivity like some caffeinated hamster on a wheel. Instead, it's about being intentionally recognizing that your time is finite and treating it with the care it deserves.

"How we spend our days is, of course, how we spend our lives." —**Annie Dillard**

You don't need to overhaul your life overnight. You don't need to become a different person. You don't need to wake up at 4 AM and run a marathon before breakfast (unless that's genuinely your thing, in which case, we need to talk). What you need is a willingness to notice the gift you've been given and the courage to use it well. The rest of this book will help you do just that: reclaim your hours, find meaning in your routines, and live—rather than merely exist—on 24 hours a day.

Key Points:
- Time is a daily gift, given equally to everyone, and cannot be saved or reclaimed once spent
- We often neglect how we use our time, assuming more will be available later
- The real challenge is to make the most of the time we have right now, not to find more
- Intentional mindful use of time leads to a more fulfilling life
- Even billionaires can't buy extra hours—time is the ultimate democracy

2. Beyond the To-Do List

> *"Beware the barrenness of a busy life."* —**Socrates**

Most of us live by a to-do list—whether it's scribbled on a sticky note, stored in an app, or mentally catalogued in that slightly panicked part of our brain that wakes us up at 3 AM. We move from one obligation to the next, checking off boxes and feeling a fleeting sense of accomplishment. Yet, even on our most productive days, there's often a lingering sense that something is missing. We wonder if life is meant to be more than just a series of checkmarks and completed errands.

This feeling isn't a flaw; it's a sign of something deeper. It's your soul gently tapping you on the shoulder and whispering, "Excuse me, but is this it?" The desire to exceed your programme, to do more than simply fulfill obligations, is a natural part of being human. It's the quiet urge to make space for curiosity, creativity, and growth, even when your calendar looks like a game of Tetris played by a sadist.

> *"The trouble with the rat race is that even if you win, you're still a rat."* —**Lily Tomlin**

The to-do list is a tool for survival, not fulfillment. It keeps the wheels turning, the bills paid, and the boss happy, but it doesn't satisfy the deeper hunger for meaning. That's why, even when you're caught up, you might feel you're falling behind in a more important way—like winning at Monopoly while losing at life.

The solution isn't to add more tasks or hustle harder. (If hustle culture was the answer, we'd all be enlightened by now, instead of just exhausted.) Instead, recognize that the urge to do more is about quality, not quantity. It's about carving out even a small space in your day for something that matters to you—something that isn't strictly necessary, but feels deeply important. Something that makes you feel like a human being rather than a human doing.

> *"Tell me, what is it you plan to do with your one wild and precious life?"* —**Mary Oliver**

You don't need to make dramatic changes or chase after grand ambitions. You don't need to quit your job and become a yoga instructor in Bali (though if that's calling you, namaste and godspeed). Start by noticing what excites you, what sparks your interest, what makes time seem to disappear in the good way. Give yourself permission to pursue it, even if only for a few minutes each day. Don't wait for the perfect moment; it rarely arrives, and when it does, it's usually wearing a disguise.

Remember, the goal isn't to be busier, but to be more alive. The desire to go beyond your to-do list is an invitation to claim a piece of your day for yourself, a chance to live, not just exist.

Key Points:
- The to-do list helps us survive, but doesn't fulfill our deeper needs for meaning and growth
- The urge to do more is natural and should be acknowledged, not dismissed
- Focus on quality over quantity—make space for what matters, even in small ways
- Don't wait for the perfect time; start where you are with what you have
- The goal is to feel more alive, not simply more productive
- Your inbox will refill itself anyway—might as well do something meaningful

After all, nobody's tombstone ever read, "Here lies John: He cleared his inbox."

3. Start Small, Stay Realistic

"A journey of a thousand miles begins with a single step—and usually a stumble." — **Lao Tzu** *(with editorial liberties)*

By now, you may be feeling a surge of motivation, a glimmer of hope that perhaps, with the right approach, you can finally "get it together." Maybe you're picturing yourself rising at dawn, conquering tasks, and still having time to meditate before breakfast.

Pause right there. Before you buy a new alarm clock, a bullet journal, and many more self-help books, let's talk about the real first step: managing your expectations and preparing for the reality of change.

"Everyone has a plan until they get punched in the mouth." —**Mike Tyson**

The impulse to overhaul your life is a powerful one, but it's also a trap—like a New Year's resolution on steroids. The fantasy of instant transformation is seductive, yet it's the surest way to disappointment. The truth is, there is no secret shortcut, no magical system, and no app that will painlessly turn you into a master of time. Despite what Silicon Valley wants you to believe, you cannot "hack" your way to enlightenment.

The journey to using your 24 hours well is not a sprint—it's a slow, sometimes clumsy, walk. Think less "Olympic athlete" and more "baby giraffe learning to stand."

"Be not afraid of going slowly; be afraid only of standing still." —**Chinese Proverb**

The first precaution is to accept that this will be difficult. Not impossible, not joyless, but genuinely challenging—like assembling IKEA furniture with missing instructions and extra parts that don't seem to belong anywhere. You're not just rearranging your schedule; you're attempting to change habits that have been years in the making. Habits, as anyone who's tried to quit caffeine or start flossing knows, are stubborn creatures. They resist change with the determination of a cat avoiding a bath.

It's tempting to believe that with enough enthusiasm, you can leap straight into a new way of living. Enthusiasm is wonderful, but it's also fickle—like a fair-weather friend who disappears at the first sign of rain. Many a grand project has died after a week because it demanded too much, too soon. The key is to start with small, manageable changes—tiny victories that build momentum and confidence. Think "light drizzle" rather than "torrential downpour."

> *"Little strokes fell great oaks."* —**Benjamin Franklin**

But don't let your initial excitement trick you into overcommitting. Ambition is good, but over-ambition is fatal—it's the difference between a challenging hike and attempting to climb Everest in flip-flops. If you try to reclaim every wasted minute, you'll quickly find yourself exhausted and discouraged. Instead, aim for modest, sustainable progress. Set a goal so small it almost feels trivial, let's call it **The 2-Minute Start.** Choose your first small step:

- Reading: Read one page, not one chapter
- Exercise: Put on workout clothes, don't commit to working out
- Meditation: Sit quietly for 2 minutes, not 20
- Writing: Write one sentence, not one page

Track only completion, not quality or quantity. Do this for 7 days before increasing.

Yes, it might feel like you're barely doing anything. That's the point. You're building a foundation, not a skyscraper.

Allow for setbacks and accidents. Life will interfere, and you will stumble. Your cat will knock over your coffee onto your journal. Your kids will decide that your meditation time is the perfect moment for an urgent discussion about dinosaurs. Your boss will schedule a meeting during your planned reading hour. That's not a sign of failure; it's a sign you're human (and possibly that you need to train your cat better).

> *"Ever tried. Ever failed. No matter. Try again. Fail again. Fail better."* —**Samuel Beckett**

Another essential precaution: don't expect to keep your old life exactly as it is and simply "add" new, productive habits on top, like productivity sprinkles on the ice cream sundae of your existence. Every positive change requires a trade-off. If you decide to spend thirty minutes a day learning something new, that's thirty minutes you won't spend on something else. Be honest about what you're willing to give up. Maybe it's a bit of TV, maybe it's scrolling through your phone, or maybe it's just the habit of staring at the wall while existentially pondering the meaning of it all.

So, before you rush out to reinvent your entire routine, pause and prepare. Accept that the road will be bumpy, that progress will be slow, and that some days will feel like you're going backwards. But also know that every small, consistent effort counts. Over time, these efforts add up to real, lasting change—not because you made one grand leap, but because you took many small, steady steps. And occasionally tripped. And got back up. And probably tripped again.

Key Points:

- Accept that changing how you use your time is genuinely challenging—there is no easy shortcut
- Don't let initial enthusiasm lead you to over-commit; start with small, manageable changes
- Allow for setbacks and be kind to yourself when they happen; persistence is more important than perfection
- Every positive change requires a trade-off—be honest about what you're willing to give up
- Begin now, however imperfectly; small, consistent efforts are the foundation of lasting progress
- Your cat will definitely interfere with your plans—accept this universal truth

4. Work Isn't Your Whole Life

> *"No one ever said on their deathbed, 'I wish I'd spent more time at the office.'"* —**Harold Kushner**

Take a moment to consider how you see your day. For many, the "workday" is the main event, the centerpiece around which everything else is arranged—like a mediocre painting in an expensive frame. The hours spent at your job—whether in an office, a shop, or hunched over a laptop in your kitchen—are treated as the day itself, while the time before and after is mere preparation or recovery. This attitude is so common that we rarely question it. It's like assuming the commercials are the main reason to watch TV.

Yet, it's precisely this mindset that leads to the nagging sense that life is passing by, unfulfilled, like being stuck in an eternal waiting room.

> *"Your work is going to fill a large part of your life, and the only way to be truly satisfied is to do what you believe is great work. And the only way to do great work is to love what you do."* —**Steve Jobs**

That's lovely advice, Steve, but most of us aren't designing the next iPhone.

Let's look at a typical scenario: You wake up, rush through your morning like you're being chased by bees, commute to work while checking emails (because apparently, urgency follows us everywhere now), and spend the bulk of your energy on your job. When the workday ends, you feel entitled to collapse into leisure, convinced you've "earned" the right to disengage. The evening becomes a blur of passive activities—scrolling through social media (looking at other people's curated lives), snacking on things you'll regret tomorrow, watching shows you won't remember next week, and waiting for the next day to begin. Rinse and repeat until retirement, at which point you'll finally have time to... remember what you wanted to do with your time.

> *"Work is a necessary evil to be avoided."* —**Mark Twain**

Now, Twain might have been a bit extreme, but he had a point. This approach is not only limiting but also illogical. If you view your job as the sum total of your day, you're surrendering most of your waking hours to something that, for many, is more duty than passion. Even if you enjoy your work (and if you do, congratulations—you're part of a fortunate minority), it's unlikely to satisfy every aspect of your curiosity, creativity, or need for connection. And if you don't enjoy your work, then you're letting the least fulfilling part of your day define your entire existence. It's like judging a meal by the Brussels sprouts.

The truth is, your time outside of work is not just a margin—it's a vital, expansive part of your life. These hours are yours to shape, free from the demands of your job. They are the space where you can pursue interests, nurture relationships, and invest in your well-being. They're also where you can finally learn to play the ukulele, though your neighbors might have opinions about that.

> *"Time you enjoy wasting is not wasted time."* **—Bertrand Russell**

This shift isn't just philosophical; it's practical. When you begin to value your non-working hours, you open up opportunities for growth and satisfaction that your job may never provide. You can learn something new, engage in a hobby, spend quality time with loved ones, or simply rest in a way that feels restorative rather than guilty. These activities aren't just "nice to have"—they are essential to living a balanced, meaningful life. They're what make you interesting at parties (remember those?).

Of course, old habits die hard—usually kicking and screaming. It's easy to fall into the trap of thinking you're too tired after work to do anything but binge-watch shows about people renovating houses you'll never afford. But consider this: when you have something to look forward to—dinner with friends, a class, a creative project—you often find reserves of energy you didn't know you had. It's like discovering a $20 bill in your pocket, but for enthusiasm.

> *"The time to relax is when you don't have time for it."* **—Sydney J. Harris**

To break the cycle, start by making a conscious decision to treat your evenings and mornings as valuable. Plan them with the same care you give your workday—though hopefully with less PowerPoint. Set aside time for activities that matter to you, even if it's just a few minutes at first. Protect this time from the encroachment of work emails, chores, and mindless distractions. Make it sacred, a non-negotiable part of your routine. Your work emails can wait. Despite what your anxiety tells you, the company will not collapse if you don't respond immediately to that message about the TPS reports.

Remember, your job is just one part of your life. It may provide income, structure, and even satisfaction, but it cannot—and should not—be expected to fulfill every need. The rest of your time is yours to claim. Don't let it slip away unnoticed like coins through a hole in your pocket.

Key Points:
- Don't let your job define your entire day; your non-working hours are equally valuable
- Reclaim your time outside work by treating it as essential, not just leftover
- Use your free hours intentionally for rest, growth, and connection—not just passive

    recovery
Start small, protect your personal time, and make it reflect your true interests and values
A balanced life requires seeing yourself as more than just a worker
Your work emails can wait—civilization won't crumble without your immediate response

5. Leisure That Nourishes

"Leisure is the mother of philosophy." —Thomas Hobbes

After a long day, it's tempting to believe that leisure is simply the absence of work—a time to switch off, zone out, and recover. It's the adult equivalent of naptime, minus the juice boxes. But not all leisure is created equal. There's a world of difference between activities that truly nourish you and those that merely fill the time, like the difference between a home-cooked meal and gas station sushi.

Many people claim exhaustion as the reason for their evening inertia. "I'm too tired to do anything but watch TV," they say, usually while simultaneously scrolling through their phone. It's multitasking, but for exhaustion. Yet, these same people will muster energy for a special event, a night out, or a favorite hobby. Suddenly, the person who was "too tired" to read a book is doing the salsa at midnight. The truth is, when you're genuinely interested in something, you often find the motivation to participate, no matter how tired you thought you were. Fatigue, in many cases, is as much mental as physical—it's often just boredom wearing a disguise.

"The cure for boredom is curiosity. There is no cure for curiosity." —Dorothy Parker

The challenge is to distinguish between leisure that restores and leisure that numbs. Passive activities—endless scrolling through feeds of people you don't really know doing things you don't really care about, channel surfing through 500 options only to conclude there's "nothing on," or mindless snacking on foods that would horrify your doctor—can feel restful in the moment but rarely leave you feeling refreshed or fulfilled. They're the junk food of leisure: momentarily satisfying but ultimately leaving you hungry for something more substantial.

In contrast, engaging in something that sparks your curiosity or creativity can actually replenish your energy, even if it requires a bit of effort to get started. It's like exercise, nobody wants to do it, but everyone feels better afterward.

"Recreation is not being idle; it is easing the wearied part by change of occupation." — **Arthur Conan Doyle**

So, what does nourishing leisure look like?

For one week, track your evening activities:
1. Activity: What did you do?

2. Duration: How long?
3. Energy after: More tired or more energized? (Rate 1-10)
4. Satisfaction: Glad you did it or wish you'd done something else?

After a week, identify patterns. Which activities consistently leave you energized (7+) and satisfied? Schedule more of these.

It's different for everyone, which is both liberating and slightly annoying, there's no one-size-fits-all solution. For some, it's reading a good book that doesn't involve vampires or self-help gurus. For others, it's learning a new skill, like cooking something more ambitious than cereal, or practicing a hobby that doesn't involve a screen. It might be spending time with friends who make you laugh until your sides hurt, playing music badly but enthusiastically, or exploring the outdoors without posting about it on Instagram.

The key is that the activity feels meaningful to you—it draws you in, holds your attention (remember that quaint concept?), and leaves you feeling more alive rather than more numb. It's the difference between watching your eighth straight episode of a show you're not even enjoying and doing something that makes you lose track of time in the good way.

> *"The time you enjoy wasting is not wasted time."* —**Bertrand Russell** *(worth repeating)*

To make room for this kind of leisure, you may need to be intentional about your evenings. Rather than letting the hours drift by like leaves on a pond (poetic, but unproductive), plan ahead. Choose one or two activities that genuinely interest you and set aside time for them, even if it's just an hour a couple of times a week. Treat these appointments with yourself as seriously as you would any other commitment—more seriously than you treat your dental appointments, at least.

It's also important to recognize that leisure is not a luxury; it's a necessity. It's not the dessert of life; it's part of the main course. A well-chosen leisure activity can act as a reset button, helping you return to your responsibilities with renewed focus and enthusiasm. It can also be a source of personal growth, connection, and joy—things that spreadsheets rarely provide.

> *"All work and no play makes Jack a dull boy."* —**Proverb** *(also, a creepy movie scene)*

Of course, you don't need to fill every evening with structured activity. That way lies madness and a color-coded calendar that would make even the most organized person weep. Balance is important. Some nights, you may simply need to rest, and that's perfectly valid. The human body is not a machine, despite what productivity gurus tell you. The goal is to be mindful about how you spend your leisure time—to choose activities that leave you feeling better, not just distracted.

If you're not sure where to start, think back to what you enjoyed as a child, before adulting crushed your spirit. Or consider what you find yourself drawn to when you have a rare free moment and aren't paralyzed by choice. Experiment with different activities until you find something that resonates. Remember, the point is not to become an expert or achieve perfection (leave that to the overachievers), but to engage with life outside of work in a way that feels meaningful to you.

Protect your leisure time from interruptions and distractions. Turn off notifications—yes, all of them. The world will not end if you don't immediately see that someone liked your photo from 2017. Set boundaries with work, and let those around you know that this time is important. Over time, you'll find that even a small investment in nourishing leisure can have a big impact on your overall well-being. You might even start to look forward to your evenings instead of just enduring them.

Key Points:
- Not all leisure is equal; choose activities that restore and engage you, not just distract
- Fatigue is often mental as well as physical; genuine interest can overcome tiredness
- Plan and protect your leisure time as you would any other important commitment
- Balance structured activity with true rest; the goal is fulfillment, not busyness
- Nourishing leisure is a necessity for well-being, not a luxury
- Your notifications can wait—Instagram will survive without you for an hour

6. Self-Compassion and Flexibility

> *"Be gentle with yourself. You are a child of the universe no less than the trees and the stars; you have a right to be here."* —**Max Ehrmann**

When you set out to reclaim your time and live more intentionally, it's easy to imagine that discipline alone will carry you through. You might picture yourself waking up early, ticking off each new habit with military precision, and never missing a beat. You'll be like one of those people in motivational videos who seem to have their life together while dramatic music plays in the background. Spoiler alert: those people also have bad days, they just don't film them.

But real life, as you know, is rarely so tidy. It's more like trying to fold a fitted sheet—theoretically possible, but mostly just frustrating and wrinkled.

> *"Life is what happens when you're busy making other plans."* —**John Lennon**

First, acknowledge your own humanity. You are not a machine, despite what your performance review might suggest. Some days you'll wake up energized and inspired, ready to conquer your carefully planned schedule. Other days you'll wake up feeling like you've been hit by a truck driven by your responsibilities. This is not a flaw—it's simply the reality of being human. Expecting yourself to operate at peak performance every day is like expecting your houseplants to bloom year-round. It's unrealistic and slightly cruel to the houseplants.

The temptation to overhaul your life in one grand gesture is strong, like the urge to cut your own hair at 2 AM. But it's also a trap. Sustainable change is gradual, like erosion but hopefully more positive. The key is gradual progress. Maybe you dedicate just half an hour a few times a week to something that matters to you. As you build confidence and momentum, you can expand your efforts. Consistency, not intensity, is the real key to progress. A little, done regularly, will always outlast a lot, done once in a burst of enthusiasm fueled by too much coffee and a TED talk.

> *"Rest when you're weary. Refresh and renew yourself, your body, your mind, your spirit. Then get back to work."* —**Ralph Marston**

Rest is not a luxury—it's a necessity. If you try to fill every moment with activity, you'll quickly burn out faster than a cheap candle. Instead, schedule regular breaks and unstructured time. Consider taking one day each week with no formal commitments—a day to do whatever you feel like, even if that's absolutely nothing. This kind of rest isn't laziness; it's a vital part of maintaining your energy and motivation for the long haul. Think of it as strategic laziness.

Setbacks are inevitable. Life will throw unexpected demands your way, like a cosmic game of dodgeball where the balls are made of obligations. Or you'll simply have days when you don't feel up to your plans—when the couch's gravitational pull is too strong to resist. When this happens, don't berate yourself or give up. Instead, treat each setback as a learning opportunity, like a very annoying teacher. Ask yourself what went wrong, what you might do differently next time, and then move on. The goal is not perfection, but progress. Even GPS recalculates when you miss a turn.

> *"The curious paradox is that when I accept myself just as I am, then I can change."* — **Carl Rogers**

Flexibility means being willing to revise your plans as you go. If you discover that your 5 AM meditation routine is just making you resentful and sleepy, don't be afraid to change it. Maybe you're not a morning person. Maybe you're barely an afternoon person. That's okay. Your needs and interests will evolve, and your approach should evolve with them. There's no shame in adjusting your course; in fact, it's a sign of wisdom and self-awareness. Rigid plans break; flexible ones bend and adapt.

Celebrate your successes, no matter how small. Did you read for ten minutes instead of immediately opening social media? Victory! Did you take a walk instead of taking a nap? Champion! Every step you take toward reclaiming your time is an achievement. Acknowledge your progress and use it as fuel to keep going. Over time, these small victories will add up to significant change, like compound interest but for your soul.

> *"And now that you don't have to be perfect, you can be good."* —*John Steinbeck*

Remember, the journey to a more intentional life is not a straight line. It's more like a child's drawing of a line—creative, meandering, and occasionally doubling back on itself. It's a process of trial and error, adjustment and growth. Be kind to yourself along the way. Self-compassion and flexibility are not just nice-to-haves—they are the very foundation of lasting fulfillment. Without them, you're just punishing yourself with productivity.

Some practical advice: Keep a "Good Enough" list alongside your "To-Do" list. Set minimum viable goals for difficult days. If your goal is to exercise for 30 minutes but you're exhausted, even a 5-minute walk counts. If you planned to read a chapter but can only manage a page, that's still reading. The "Good Enough" list reminds you that something is better than nothing, and that showing up imperfectly is better than not showing up at all.

Key Points:
- Accept your humanity—expect ups and downs, and adjust your plans accordingly
- Begin with small, manageable steps; consistency is more important than intensity
- Schedule regular rest and unstructured time to avoid burnout
- Treat setbacks as learning opportunities, not failures
- Stay flexible and be willing to revise your plans as your needs evolve
- Celebrate every step forward, no matter how small
- Perfect is the enemy of good—and good is good enough

7. Focus in a Distracted World

"The successful warrior is the average man with laser-like focus." —**Bruce Lee**

In today's world, distractions are everywhere. Notifications ping with the persistence of a woodpecker on espresso. Emails pile up like dishes in a bachelor's sink. The lure of endless scrolling is always just a swipe away, promising you'll find something interesting after just one more video of someone falling off a skateboard. The ability to focus your mind on a single task can feel almost impossible—like trying to meditate in the middle of a Black Friday sale.

But here's the thing: without focus, even the best intentions dissolve into a haze of half-finished thoughts and wasted hours. You end up with 47 browser tabs open, three partially written emails, and the vague feeling that you were supposed to be doing something important. What was it again?

"Where focus goes, energy flows and results show." —**Tony Robbins**

The good news is that focus is not a mysterious talent reserved for monks, chess masters, and people who can actually finish a book. It's a skill, and like any skill, it can be developed with practice. The first step is to recognize that you do have control over your attention, even if it doesn't always feel that way. Your mind may wander like a tourist without a map, but you can gently guide it back—again and again. Think of it as training a very distractible puppy. A puppy that's obsessed with cat videos.

Begin by using small, everyday moments to practice focus. Your commute (assuming you're not driving—please don't practice focus while operating heavy machinery), a walk to the store, or even waiting in line can become opportunities for mental training. Pick something simple to focus on: your breathing, the sensation of walking, or a specific question you want to think through. When your mind inevitably wanders to that embarrassing thing you did in 2012, just notice it and bring your attention back. No judgment, no frustration—just a gentle redirect, like a GPS that doesn't judge you for missing the exit.

"The secret of change is to focus all of your energy not on fighting the old, but on building the new." —**Socrates**

This isn't about shutting out the world or becoming a monk (unless that's your thing—no judgment). It's about learning to guide your thoughts, rather than letting them be pulled in every direction like a dog walker with seventeen enthusiastic puppies. When you practice focus, you'll find that your mind becomes less prone to worry, less susceptible to distraction, and more capable of sustained effort—whether you're working, learning, or simply enjoying a conversation without checking your phone every thirty seconds.

You don't need elaborate rituals or special equipment. You don't need to buy a meditation cushion, burn incense, or chant in Sanskrit (though again, if that's your jam, jam on). The only requirement is a willingness to try, and the patience to persist when your mind inevitably rebels. Because it will rebel. Your brain has gotten very comfortable being distracted, thank you very much, and it's not going to give up without a fight.

> *"Concentration is the secret of strength."* —**Ralph Waldo Emerson**

If you want to deepen this practice, try focusing on something useful. Read a short passage from a philosopher like Marcus Aurelius or Epictetus in the evening—or if philosophy isn't your speed, literally any text that requires more than three seconds of attention. Spend your commute the next morning reflecting on it. Or choose a problem you want to solve, and use your spare moments to turn it over in your mind like a Rubik's cube, but hopefully less frustrating. The subject matters less than the act of sustained attention.

Here's a practical exercise: Set a timer for just five minutes.

THE FOCUS LADDER: Building Attention Gradually

Week 1: Single-Point Focus (5 minutes daily)
- Choose object (candle flame, photo, plant)
- When mind wanders, note "thinking" and return to object
- Count wanderings without judgment

Week 2: Breath Counting (7 minutes daily)
- Count breaths 1-10, repeat
- Lost count? Start at 1
- Goal: Complete three full cycles

Week 3: Productive Focus (10 minutes daily)
- Choose one task (reading, writing, planning)
- No devices in reach
- If distracted, mark tally on paper, continue

Week 4: Deep Work Trial (15 minutes daily)
- Complex task requiring thought
- Phone in another room
- One specific outcome to achieve

Success = Consistency, not perfection

Choose one task; reading, writing, or even just sitting and thinking about a specific topic. When your mind wanders (not if, when), gently bring it back. No phones, no notifications, no "quick checks" of anything. Just five minutes. It will feel like an eternity the first time. That's normal. You're basically doing push-ups for your attention span.

> *"You will never reach your destination if you stop and throw stones at every dog that barks." —Winston Churchill*

Don't be discouraged by setbacks. Everyone struggles with focus, especially in a world designed to steal your attention and sell it to advertisers. The important thing is to keep practicing. Each time you bring your mind back, you're strengthening your ability to concentrate. It's like going to the gym, but without the awkward small talk and mysterious stains on the equipment.

Over time, you'll find that improved focus spills over into every area of your life. You'll worry less (though probably not about that thing from 2012—that's apparently permanent). You'll accomplish more without feeling frantic. You'll experience greater satisfaction in your work and relationships. You'll actually remember what you read, instead of realizing three pages later that you have no idea what just happened. Focus is not just a productivity tool—it's a path to a richer, more intentional life.

Key Points:

- Focus is a skill that can be developed through practice
- Use everyday moments to train your attention, bringing your mind back when it wanders
- The act of returning your focus is the exercise—don't be discouraged by distractions
- Start small—even five minutes of focused attention is valuable
- Deepening your focus improves every area of life, from work to relationships to personal growth
- Your brain will resist at first—that's normal and not a sign you're doing it wrong

8. Daily Self-Check-In

*"The unexamined life is not worth living." —**Socrates** (who clearly never had to examine his life while dealing with a WiFi outage)*

Once you've begun to harness your attention, the next step is to use it for self-examination. In a world obsessed with external achievement—LinkedIn updates, Instagram likes, and whatever fresh hell Twitter has become—it's easy to overlook the importance of looking inward. Yet, real fulfillment comes from understanding yourself: your motivations, your habits, and the gap between your actions and your values. You know, that gap that sometimes feels more like a canyon.

Set aside a few minutes each day, perhaps during your commute home or before bed (or while hiding in the bathroom from your responsibilities), to reflect on how you spent your time. Ask yourself: Did I act in line with my principles, or did I spend three hours arguing with strangers on the internet about pineapple on pizza? What moments brought me satisfaction? Where did I fall short, and why? Was it worth getting worked up about that email, or could I have just let it go?

*"Know thyself." —**Ancient Greek aphorism** (probably written by someone who didn't have to know themselves through social media)*

This isn't about self-criticism or guilt—save that for when you remember embarrassing moments at 3 AM like the rest of us. It's about honest assessment and gentle course correction. Think of it as a GPS recalculation for your soul. You're not berating yourself for taking a wrong turn; you're simply finding a better route.

You might find it helpful to keep a journal, jotting down thoughts or patterns you notice. Don't worry about making it Instagram-worthy with perfect handwriting and artistic doodles. This isn't for show; it's for growth. Or simply take a quiet walk and let your mind wander over the events of the day—though maybe leave your phone behind so it doesn't wander onto social media instead. The goal is not to obsess over mistakes (leave that for your anxiety to handle), but to cultivate a habit of self-awareness.

> *"At the end of the day, ask yourself: 'Did I make a difference or just a living?'"* — **Unknown**

Here are some questions to consider during your daily check-in:
- What did I do today that I'm proud of?
- What did I do that I wish I'd handled differently?
- Did I spend my time on things that matter to me, or did I get hijacked by urgency?
- What patterns do I notice in my behavior?
- Am I becoming the person I want to be, or just a more tired version of who I was yesterday?

THE 3-MINUTE EVENING REVIEW

Set phone timer for 3 minutes. Write continuously:

- One thing I'm grateful for today
- One thing I learned about myself
- One intention for tomorrow

No editing, no perfection. When timer ends, you're done. Do this for 30 days to build the habit.

Books and mentors can provide guidance, but no one knows your life as intimately as you do—not even your FBI agent. The daily self-check-in is your opportunity to become your own guide, to notice where you're growing and where you need support. It's a small investment of time with a profound payoff: greater clarity, resilience, and satisfaction. Plus, it's cheaper than therapy (though not a replacement for it—seriously, therapy is great).

> *"The most important conversations you'll ever have are the ones you have with yourself."* —*David Goggins*

Don't worry about getting it perfect. The act of reflecting regularly is more important than any particular insight you might gain. Some days, your mind will be clear and focused, offering profound revelations about your life's purpose. Other days, your deepest insight will be, "I should not have eaten that gas station sushi." Both are valid. That's normal. The key is to keep showing up, to make self-reflection a habit rather than an occasional event, like flossing but for your psyche.

As you continue this practice, you'll begin to notice patterns—habits that serve you, and habits that hold you back like that friend who always wants to go to karaoke. You'll become more attuned to your own needs and desires, and more capable of making choices that align with your values. You might notice that you always feel drained after certain activities or energized after others. Use this information. It's data about your life, and unlike most data, it's actually useful.

> *"Be yourself; everyone else is already taken."* —**Oscar Wilde**

Over time, this self-awareness will help you live more intentionally, with greater purpose and satisfaction. You'll spend less time on things that don't matter and more time on things that do. You'll make decisions based on your values rather than your impulses. You'll probably still argue about pineapple on pizza occasionally, but at least you'll know why.

Remember, the goal is not to become your own harshest critic but to become your own best ally. Use your daily self-check-in as a time to encourage yourself, to celebrate your progress (however small), and to gently steer yourself back on course when you stray. Be the friend to yourself that you are to others; supportive, understanding, and only occasionally sarcastic.

Key Points:

- Regular self-reflection helps align your actions with your values
- Use a few minutes each day for honest, non-judgmental assessment
- Ask yourself meaningful questions about how you spent your time and energy
- Journaling or quiet contemplation can deepen your self-understanding
- Self-awareness leads to better decisions and greater fulfillment
- Be your own ally, not your harshest critic—you already have the internet for that

9. Feed Your Curiosity

"I have no special talent. I am only passionately curious." —**Albert Einstein**

Many people believe that meaningful personal growth requires a passion for literature, a deep engagement with the arts, or at least the ability to discuss wine without using the word "grape-y." They imagine they need to become the sort of person who goes to gallery openings and nods knowingly at abstract sculptures that look suspiciously like someone dropped their lunch. In reality, curiosity is the only prerequisite. Whether your interests lie in music, painting, architecture, science, or even the surprisingly complex mechanics of how your coffee maker works, there's a world of knowledge waiting to be explored.

Don't be discouraged if you don't consider yourself "artistic" or "cultured." Those are just words people use to feel superior at dinner parties. The goal is not to become an expert who can bore people with obscure facts (though that's a delightful side effect). The goal is to open yourself to new experiences and ideas, to stretch your perspective and find joy in discovery. It's about becoming someone who says "I wonder..." more often than "I know."

"The cure for boredom is curiosity. There is no cure for curiosity." —**Ellen Parr**

Start small. Rome wasn't built in a day, and neither was that person at parties who somehow knows about both cryptocurrency and contemporary dance. Choose one area that intrigues you, and make it a regular part of your week. Read a beginner's guide without shame—everyone starts somewhere. Listen to a podcast while pretending to work. Join a local group, even if you're the person who knows the least. Especially if you're the person who knows the least. You don't need to impress anyone or achieve mastery; your only job is to be curious and receptive. Think of yourself as a tourist in the land of new knowledge—enthusiastic, slightly confused, but eager to learn.

Here are some ways to feed your curiosity without overwhelming yourself:

> Visit a museum and spend time with just ONE piece that catches your eye
> Watch a documentary about something you know nothing about
> Take a free online course in something completely unrelated to your job
> Ask someone about their hobby and actually listen to the answer
> Read the Wikipedia page of something you've always wondered about
> Go to a lecture at your local library (they still exist!)

> *"The important thing is not to stop questioning."* —**Albert Einstein** *(again—the man really liked curiosity)*

Over time, you'll find that your curiosity spills over into other areas of your life like an enthusiastically overfilled coffee cup. You'll notice more, appreciate more, and feel more connected to the wider world. You'll become the person who says "Did you know..." at parties, which is annoying but also kind of endearing. This is not just enrichment—it's nourishment for your mind and spirit. It's the difference between existing in the world and engaging with it.

If you're not sure where to start, think back to what fascinated you as a child, before practicality murdered your sense of wonder. Did you collect rocks? Love dinosaurs? Want to be an astronaut? That enthusiasm is still in there somewhere, probably hanging out with your ability to stay up past 11 PM. Dust it off. See if it still fits.

> *"Anyone who stops learning is old, whether at twenty or eighty. Anyone who keeps learning stays young."* —**Henry Ford**

Protect your curiosity time from interruptions and distractions. Turn off notifications; the internet will still be there when you get back. Set boundaries with work, your employer bought your time, not your soul. Let those around you know that this time is important. It's not "doing nothing," it's "becoming more interesting."

The beautiful thing about curiosity is that it compounds. The more you learn, the more connections you see. The more connections you see, the more interested you become. Before you know it, you're the person who can explain why Van Gogh only sold one painting in his lifetime AND why octopi have three hearts. (Spoiler: Life is hard when you're Van Gogh, and octopi need backup hearts for all that incredible shape-shifting.)

> *"Wonder is the beginning of wisdom."* —**Socrates**

Remember, feeding your curiosity isn't about becoming a walking encyclopedia or winning pub trivia (though that's a nice bonus). It's about staying engaged with life, maintaining your sense of wonder, and remembering that there's always more to discover. In a world that often feels like it's on repeat, curiosity is your escape hatch into the extraordinary.

Key Points:

- Curiosity is the key to personal growth and fulfillment, not expertise
- You don't need to be "cultured"—just interested
- Start small and make curiosity a regular habit, not a rare event
- Explore new subjects or experiences, even if you know nothing about them
- Protect your curiosity time like you'd protect your WiFi password
- The more you learn, the more interesting the world becomes
- You're never too old to wonder why things are the way they are

10. Nothing in Life is Humdrum

> *"The world is full of magic things, patiently waiting for our senses to grow sharper."* — **W.B. Yeats**

It's easy to look at the daily grind and think, "Is this all there is?" The routine, the repetitive tasks, the seemingly dull moments—they can make life feel monotonous, as if you're just shuffling from one obligation to the next like a very responsible zombie. You wake up, commute, work, commute, eat something questionable, watch something forgettable, sleep, repeat. If life were a movie, this would be the montage they'd use to show time passing meaninglessly.

But what if the ordinary is simply waiting for you to see it differently? What if the humdrum is actually full of hidden interest and meaning, waiting to be uncovered by a curious mind? What if your life is actually fascinating and you're just not paying attention?

> *"There are only two ways to live your life. One is as though nothing is a miracle. The other is as though everything is a miracle."* —**Albert Einstein** (the man was quotable)

The secret to transforming the mundane into the fascinating lies in understanding cause and effect. Everything that happens around you is part of a chain of events, a story unfolding in real time. It's like being in a mystery novel where you're both the detective and a character. When you start to see the connections—the reasons behind why things are the way they are—you begin to appreciate the complexity and beauty of everyday life.

Take your daily commute, for example. It might seem like a tedious journey, a necessary evil between bed and desk. But it's actually a microcosm of society. The traffic jams are a real-time physics experiment in flow dynamics. The people you see are each living their own complex stories—that person running for the bus might be late for a job interview that could change their life. The infrastructure that supports your route is the result of decades of urban planning, political decisions, and engineering marvels that would have seemed like magic a century ago.

> *"To see a World in a Grain of Sand / And a Heaven in a Wild Flower"* —**William Blake**

Or consider your job. Even if it feels dull on the surface (and let's be honest, most jobs have their moments of pure tedium), there's a story behind it. Why does your company exist? Someone had an idea, took a risk, probably failed a few times, and somehow created something that now employs you. How does your role fit into the bigger picture? What are the forces shaping your industry? That boring meeting about quarterly reports? It's actually about human beings trying to make sense of chaos, to find patterns and meaning in numbers. It's poetry, just with more spreadsheets.

Even the most mundane objects have fascinating stories. Your coffee mug? Someone designed it, choosing that exact curve of the handle. It was manufactured, possibly halfway around the world, shipped across oceans, stocked on a shelf, until you picked it. Now it's part of your daily ritual, holding the liquid that makes mornings bearable. That's globalization, design, commerce, and human comfort all in one ceramic vessel.

> *"If you look the right way, you can see that the whole world is a garden."* —**Frances Hodgson Burnett**

Nature, too, is endlessly fascinating when you look closely. That tree you pass every day? It's conducting complex chemical processes, communicating with other trees through underground networks, and providing homes for countless creatures. It's been standing there longer than you've been alive and will probably outlast you. It's essentially a time traveler, and you walk past it eating a bagel.

The changing seasons aren't just weather patterns—they're the Earth dancing with the sun. The behavior of your pet isn't just cute or annoying—it's millions of years of evolution compressed into a creature that now depends on you for treats. Even the dust in your house has stories—dead skin cells, pollen from plants, tiny meteorite fragments. You're literally made of stardust, and so is everything else.

> *"Everything has beauty, but not everyone sees it."* —**Confucius**

The point is, nothing in life is truly dull. It's all about perspective. When you cultivate curiosity and look for the causes behind the effects, you open yourself to a richer experience. The world becomes a place of endless discovery, and your daily life gains depth and color. Even the most familiar places and routines can surprise you when you start to ask "why" and "how."

So next time you find yourself bored or restless, try to see the story behind the scene. Ask questions:
- Why do people behave the way they do? (Psychology!)
- What led to this moment? (History!)
- How do small changes ripple outward? (Chaos theory!)
- What would an alien think of this human ritual? (Anthropology!)

THE WONDER PRACTICE
Choose one routine daily activity. For one week, notice something new:
- Monday: Visual details you've missed
- Tuesday: Sounds involved
- Wednesday: Physical sensations
- Thursday: The history/origin of objects involved
- Friday: The people who made it possible
- Weekend: Connections to the larger world

Example: Making coffee → bean origins → farmers → global trade → your morning ritual's worldwide journey

> "In every walk with nature, one receives far more than he seeks." —*John Muir*

You might be surprised at how much there is to learn and appreciate, even in the most ordinary circumstances. Your breakfast is a agricultural miracle. Your smartphone is more powerful than the computers that sent humans to the moon. Your ability to read these words is the result of thousands of years of language evolution. You're surrounded by wonders; you've just gotten used to them.

Remember, the extraordinary is often hidden in the ordinary. It's waiting for you to notice. The humdrum is only humdrum if you refuse to look beneath the surface. Life is full of richness for those willing to dig a little deeper. You don't need to travel to exotic places or have extraordinary experiences—you just need to pay attention to the extraordinariness of ordinary experience.

Key Points:
    The ordinary is full of hidden interest and meaning when you look for cause and effect
    Everything around you has a story—your job, your commute, even your coffee mug
    Curiosity transforms routine experiences into opportunities for discovery
    Nature and society offer endless fascination for those who pay attention
    Ask questions about the familiar to discover the unfamiliar within it
    The extraordinary is often hidden in the ordinary—seek it out
    You're surrounded by miracles; you've just gotten used to them

11. Serious Reading

> *"A reader lives a thousand lives before he dies. The man who never reads lives only one."* —**George R.R. Martin**

Reading is often seen as a leisure activity, a way to relax or escape. It's what you do on vacation, or when the WiFi goes out. But serious reading is something different. It's an active, demanding process that challenges your mind and expands your understanding. It's about engaging deeply with ideas, not just skimming for entertainment or to find out if the butler did it (spoiler: it's always the butler, except when it isn't).

Not all reading is created equal. Novels, while enjoyable and even enlightening, often don't require the same mental effort as other forms of literature. They can carry you along like a gentle current, which is lovely when you want to relax but less helpful when you want to grow. It's the difference between floating in a pool and swimming laps—both involve water, but only one improves your cardiovascular health.

> *"I cannot remember the books I've read any more than the meals I have eaten; even so, they have made me."* —**Ralph Waldo Emerson**

Poetry, for example, is one of the highest forms of literature. It compresses meaning into a few words like a linguistic espresso shot. A poem doesn't just tell you something; it makes you work for understanding. It demands careful attention and interpretation. Reading poetry can be challenging—like trying to fold a fitted sheet while solving a Rubik's cube—but it rewards you with profound insights and emotional depth. It asks you to slow down, to savor language, and to wrestle with meaning like Jacob wrestling the angel, but with less risk of hip displacement.

If poetry feels intimidating (and let's be honest, it can feel like trying to understand your teenager's slang), try essays or philosophical works that explore ideas clearly and thoughtfully. History and philosophy offer rich material for serious reading, helping you understand the world and your place in it. These works invite you to grapple with big questions: Why are we here? What is justice? Why do hot dogs come in packages of ten but buns in packages of eight? (Okay, philosophy might not answer that last one, but it's worth pondering.)

> *"Reading furnishes the mind only with materials of knowledge; it is thinking that makes what we read ours."* —**John Locke**

The key to serious reading is focus and reflection. Don't rush through texts like you're trying to catch a train. This isn't a race, and there's no prize for finishing first except the hollow victory of not understanding what you just read. Take your time to absorb the meaning, consider the arguments, and relate them to your own experiences. Read a paragraph and then pause. What did it really say? Do you agree? Why or why not?

Keep a journal or notes to capture your thoughts and questions. Yes, this makes you one of those people who writes in margins, but embrace it. The act of writing down your reactions can deepen your understanding and help you remember what you've learned. Plus, future you will appreciate past you's insights, even if they're just "What?" and "This guy needs an editor."

> *"Some books are to be tasted, others to be swallowed, and some few to be chewed and digested."* —**Francis Bacon**

Choose a subject or author to specialize in for a period. This focus allows you to build depth and see connections between ideas. It's better to understand a few works well than to skim many superficially. Let yourself become a temporary expert on a topic. Read multiple works by the same author. Read their critics. Read their influences. Become that person who can casually drop "Well, as Kierkegaard would say..." into conversation (but please, use this power sparingly).

Here's a practical approach to serious reading:

Month 1: Essays & Articles (10 min/day)
- Choose one publication (Atlantic, Aeon, etc.)
- Read one piece fully before moving on
- Write one insight in margin or notebook

Month 2: Short Philosophy (15 min/day)
- Start with "Meditations" or "Letters from a Stoic"
- Read same passage twice
- Journal one paragraph response

Month 3: Poetry (20 min/day)
- One poem, three times
- First read: Just experience
- Second read: Notice techniques
- Third read: Personal meaning

Month 4: Full Integration
- Alternate between all three
- Share one insight weekly with someone
- Begin building personal philosophy

> *"The reading of all good books is like conversation with the finest men of past centuries."* —***Descartes***

Serious reading is not about quantity but quality. It's about cultivating your mind and enriching your life. It's a practice that requires discipline but offers lasting rewards. Over time, you'll find your thinking sharpened, your perspective broadened, and your appreciation for literature deepened. You'll also become insufferable at book clubs, but that's a small price to pay for wisdom.

So, set aside regular time for serious reading. Approach it with curiosity and commitment. Let it become a habit, a part of your routine that you look forward to—like coffee, but for your brain. The more you invest in serious reading, the more you'll get out of it—not just knowledge, but wisdom, empathy, and a richer sense of self. Plus, you'll always have something to talk about at parties besides the weather.

Key Points:
- Serious reading is an active, challenging process that deepens understanding
- Not all reading is equal; focus on works that make you think and reflect
- Poetry, essays, history, and philosophy offer rich material for growth
- Read slowly, take notes, and reflect to build real understanding
- Quality matters more than quantity; become a temporary expert rather than a permanent dilettante
- Make serious reading a regular habit—your brain will thank you
- You'll become more interesting at parties, though possibly also more pretentious

12. Dangers to Avoid

> *"The road to hell is paved with good intentions."* —**Samuel Johnson** *(who clearly tried a self-improvement program)*

As you embark on the journey of living intentionally and making the most of your time, it's important to be aware of certain pitfalls. These dangers can derail your progress and turn your efforts into burdens rather than blessings. It's like walking through a minefield, except the mines are made of self-righteousness and rigid scheduling.

One of the greatest risks is becoming a prig—a person who takes themselves too seriously and loses their sense of humor. You know the type: they corner you at parties to explain their morning routine in excruciating detail, judge your coffee choice, and use the phrase "optimize your life" without irony. It's easy to become self-righteous about your new habits and look down on others who don't share your commitment to waking up at 5 AM to journal about gratitude. This attitude not only alienates people (faster than talking about your cryptocurrency portfolio) but also saps your own joy.

> *"Blessed is he who can laugh at himself, for he shall never cease to be amused."* — **Unknown**

Remember, your time is your own. The world has been spinning long before you started managing your hours, and it will continue regardless of your success or failure. The universe is supremely indifferent to your productivity system. Don't let your program become a rigid religion that controls you instead of serving you. You're trying to improve your life, not become a time-management fundamentalist.

Another danger is obsession with schedules. When every minute is accounted for, you might find yourself anxious and stressed, always rushing to the next task like a hamster on an espresso-powered wheel. "Sorry, I can't attend your wedding—my schedule says I'm supposed to be reading Proust from 2:00 to 3:30." This can make life feel like a prison rather than a playground. A prison with color-coded calendars, but a prison nonetheless.

> *"Life is what happens when you're busy making other plans."* —**John Lennon** *(worth repeating)*

It's important to build flexibility into your routine. Allow for breaks, spontaneous moments, and even deliberate idleness. Sometimes the best moments in life come from saying "screw the schedule" and doing something unexpected. These pauses refresh your mind and keep your efforts sustainable. Remember: you're a human being, not a Swiss train schedule.

Avoid the trap of trying to do too much too soon. This is the "New Year's Resolution Syndrome," the ambitious plan that flames out by January 15th. Overloading your schedule leads to burnout and disappointment. You'll end up like Icarus, except instead of flying too close to the sun, you're trying to learn Sanskrit, master the violin, and train for a marathon simultaneously. Spoiler: your wings will still melt.

> *"The perfect is the enemy of the good."* —**Voltaire**

Here are some warning signs you've gone too far:
- You refer to spending time with friends as "social capital investment"
- You've scheduled your bathroom breaks
- You feel guilty for watching a sunset without simultaneously practicing mindfulness
- You've optimized your sleep but forgotten how to dream
- You judge others for their "inefficient" leisure choices

Finally, choose activities that genuinely interest you. Don't pursue habits just because they seem impressive or difficult. Learning ancient Greek might sound intellectual, but if you hate it, you're just punishing yourself in a dead language. Your time is precious—invest it in what brings you satisfaction and growth. There's no point in becoming a more miserable version of yourself.

> *"All work and no play makes Jack a dull boy."* —**Proverb** *(also a terrifying movie scene)*

Remember to maintain perspective. Yes, making the most of your time is important, but so is enjoying the ride. Life is not a productivity competition. There's no prize for using every second efficiently except perhaps an early grave and a really organized funeral.

By being mindful of these dangers, you can maintain balance and keep your journey enjoyable and effective. Stay humble—you're figuring this out like everyone else. Stay flexible—rigidity is the enemy of joy. And above all, keep your sense of humor. If you can't laugh at yourself for accidentally scheduling "spontaneous fun" from 3:00 to 3:30 on a Tuesday, you've already lost the plot.

> *"Angels can fly because they take themselves lightly."* —**G.K. Chesterton**

Your time is a gift—treat it as such, and you'll find that intentional living brings not just productivity, but genuine fulfillment. And if you find yourself becoming insufferable, remember: the goal was to live better, not to become someone others want to avoid at parties.

Key Points:
- Beware of becoming self-righteous or rigid about your new habits
- Don't let schedules become prisons; build in flexibility and rest
- Avoid overloading yourself; start small and grow gradually
- Choose activities that genuinely interest you, not just those that seem impressive
- Maintain perspective—life is not a productivity competition
- Keep your sense of humor; if you can't laugh at yourself, you're doing it wrong
- Your time is a gift to be enjoyed, not a resource to be maximized into misery

Epilogue: The Gentle Revolution

So here we are, you and I, at the end of our journey together—though in truth, your real journey is just beginning. You've read the chapters, considered the ideas, perhaps even tried a few experiments with your hours. Maybe you've had successes that surprised you. Almost certainly you've had setbacks that didn't.

If you came to this book seeking a final answer—a perfect system that would transform you into a master of time—you may feel disappointed. There is no such system. There never was. Time mastery is a myth sold by people who want you to buy their planners.

But if you came seeking something more modest and more profound—a shift in how you see your hours, a gentler way of being with yourself, a framework for gradual change—then perhaps you've found what you needed. Not what you wanted, but what you needed.

The truth is, you will never use your time perfectly. You will have days when you fall back into old patterns, when you scroll mindlessly for hours, when you let opportunities slip by like missed trains. You will have moments of feeling just as stuck, just as rushed, just as overwhelmed as before you picked up this book.

This is not failure. This is life.

The gentle revolution isn't about perfection. It's about progress. It's about noticing when you're drifting and kindly redirecting yourself. It's about celebrating the small victories—the evening you chose a walk over another episode, the morning you paused to actually taste your coffee, the conversation you had with full presence instead of half attention.

These moments may seem insignificant. They're not. They're the building blocks of a different kind of life—one measured not in productivity metrics or achievement lists, but in depth of experience and richness of days.

Arnold Bennett knew this truth over a century ago, and it remains unchanged: you have, and have always had, all the time there is. Twenty-four hours, every day, until your days are done. You cannot buy more, borrow more, or save some for later. But—and here's the miracle—you don't need more. You have enough. You've always had enough.

What you need is not more time but more life in your time. More presence in your moments. More intention in your choices. More kindness toward yourself when you fall short of your ideals—which you will, repeatedly, because you're beautifully, imperfectly human.

As you close this book and return to your life, remember this: every morning, you wake to a fresh start. Every evening, you can reflect without judgment. Every moment, you can choose again. The path to a meaningful life isn't a straight line but a spiral—you'll revisit the same challenges, but each time from a slightly higher vantage point.

Some days you'll feel like you're making real progress. Other days you'll feel like you're exactly where you started. Both feelings are lying to you. Change happens slowly, then suddenly. Growth is invisible until it isn't. The seeds you plant today—of awareness, of intention, of self-compassion—will bloom in their own time, not yours.

The world will not make this easy for you. It will continue to demand your attention, fragment your focus, and insist that busy equals important. It will try to convince you that your worth lies in your output, that rest is laziness, that scrolling is connection. The world is wrong about these things. You know this now.

Your task is not to fight the world but to create small sanctuaries within it. Moments of depth in the shallows. Islands of calm in the chaos. Practices that anchor you when everything else is in motion. You don't need to retreat to a monastery or quit your job or delete all your apps (though if any of those call to you, listen). You just need to remember that your hours are your own, even when they don't feel like it.

Years from now, you won't remember the emails you answered or the shows you binged or the worries that kept you awake. You'll remember the moments when you were fully alive—the sunset that stopped you in your tracks, the conversation that changed your perspective, the quiet morning when everything felt possible, the ordinary Tuesday that you decided to live extraordinarily.

These moments are available to you every day. They're hiding in plain sight, waiting for you to notice them. They don't announce themselves with fanfare. They whisper. But once you start listening, you'll hear them everywhere.

This is the 24-hour miracle: not that time can be conquered, but that it can be inhabited. Not that life can be optimized, but that it can be lived. Not that you'll become a different person, but that you'll finally become yourself—one mindful hour at a time.

The clock is ticking. It always has been. But now you know the secret: that's not a threat. It's an invitation.

Your 24 hours are waiting.

What will you do with them?

No, what will you *be* with them?

The answer to that question is your life.

Make it count. Make it yours. Make it real.

And when you forget, because you will forget, just begin again.

The miracle is always there, always patient, always ready.

Just like you.

PART 4 – FROM STRESSFUL TO SUCCESSFUL

To everyone navigating life's storms, may you find calm, clarity, and courage on your own journey.

"Out of difficulties grow miracles." — **Jean de La Bruyère**

Remember: Within each challenge is the seed of possibility, waiting to grow.

From Stressful to Successful
A Personalized Pathway to Resilience and Growth

About Things That Matter
A Self-Improvement Series for Success

Book 8

JC Ryan

Disclaimer

The information in this book is provided for educational and informational purposes only. It is not intended to be used as medical advice or as a substitute for treatment by a doctor or healthcare provider.

The information and opinions contained in this publication are believed to be accurate based on the information available to the author. However, the contents have not been evaluated by the U.S. Food and Drug Administration and are not intended to diagnose, treat, cure, or prevent disease.

The author and publisher are not responsible for the use, effectiveness, or safety of any procedure or treatment mentioned in this book. The publisher is not responsible for errors and omissions.

Warning

All treatment of any medical condition (without exception) must always be done under supervision of a qualified medical professional. The fact that a substance is "natural" does not necessarily mean that it has no side effects or interaction with other medications.

Medical professionals are qualified and experienced to give advice on side effects and interactions of all types of medication.

About This Book

From Stressful to Successful: A Personalized Pathway to Resilience and Growth is your companion for navigating life's most overwhelming events and everyday stresses. Inspired by real-life challenges and supported by psychological research, this book guides you to understand the impact of major life changes—from loss and separation to financial upheaval and unexpected transitions.

With practical tools, reflective exercises, and a step-by-step approach, you'll discover how to:

- Recognize and process the most stressful events in your life

- Build personalized strategies for managing stress and adversity

- Transform setbacks into opportunities for personal growth

- Cultivate resilience, emotional balance, and authentic self-confidence

Whether you're coping with a profound loss, adapting to new roles, or simply seeking more calm and clarity, "From Stressful to Successful" offers a clear roadmap forward. This book is part of the "About Things That Matter" series, providing readers with actionable wisdom and real support through every season of life.

Introduction: The Journey

We all know something about stress. We've all experienced it in some form—whether it's job pressures, family responsibilities, financial concerns, health challenges, or simply the feeling that there aren't enough hours in the day. Even positive experiences—a promotion, a new relationship, or personal achievement—can trigger stress responses in our bodies and minds.

While a certain amount of stress is a normal part of life, prolonged stress can lead to exhaustion, illness, and more serious health problems. It places an undue burden on many of our body's systems, especially the heart, blood vessels, adrenal glands, and immune system.

But what if there was a way to not just manage stress, but to transform it into a catalyst for success?

This book offers a fresh perspective on stress—not as an enemy to be defeated, but as a signal that can guide us toward meaningful change and growth. By understanding your unique stress profile, learning evidence-based techniques for resilience, and creating personalized strategies for thriving, you can move from merely surviving to truly succeeding.

The journey from stressful to successful isn't about eliminating all stress from your life—that would be impossible and even undesirable. Rather, it's about developing the awareness, skills, and habits that allow you to respond to life's challenges in ways that promote your well-being, purpose, and growth.

Whether you're facing career demands, relationship challenges, health concerns, or simply seeking greater balance and fulfillment, this book provides a roadmap for transforming stress into a stepping stone for success. Let's begin the journey together.

Chapter 1: What Is Stress—And Why Does It Matter?

Stress is a universal human experience—as ancient as our existence and as modern as our digital notifications. Yet despite its ubiquity, stress remains widely misunderstood. Is it a villain that undermines our health and happiness? A necessary catalyst for growth and achievement? Or perhaps something more nuanced that defies simple categorization?

The Evolution of Our Understanding

The concept of stress as we know it today is relatively recent. While humans have always experienced the physiological and psychological responses we now call "stress," it wasn't until the 1930s that endocrinologist Hans Selye—now regarded as the father of stress research—gave scientific meaning to the term.

Selye's groundbreaking work revealed that stress is not merely an emotional state but a specific biological response pattern. He observed that laboratory animals exposed to various physical and emotional stimuli exhibited similar physical changes—enlarged adrenal glands, shrinking lymphatic structures, and gastric ulcers. This led him to define stress as "the non-specific response of the body to any demand for change."

Since Selye's pioneering research, our understanding has evolved dramatically. Modern neuroscience has illuminated how stress affects brain structure and function. Psychoneuroimmunology has revealed intricate connections between our thoughts, nervous system, and immune responses. Epigenetics has shown how chronic stress can even influence gene expression, potentially affecting future generations.

Eustress vs. Distress: Not All Stress Is Created Equal

Perhaps the most important evolution in our understanding is the recognition that stress exists on a spectrum. As Selye himself noted: "Stress is not even necessarily bad for you; it is also the spice of life, for any emotion, any activity causes stress."

Eustress (positive stress) energizes and motivates. It's the butterflies before a performance, the excitement of starting a new project, or the challenge of learning a new skill. Eustress is typically:
- Short-term
- Perceived as within our coping abilities

- Feels exciting and improving
- Associated with improved performance and growth

Distress (negative stress) overwhelms and depletes. It's the crushing deadline, the persistent financial worry, or the ongoing conflict in a relationship. Distress is typically:

- Prolonged or chronic
- Perceived as beyond our coping abilities
- Feels unpleasant and anxiety-producing
- Associated with impaired performance and health problems

The difference often lies not in the stressor itself, but in our perception of and response to it. What energizes one person might overwhelm another. What feels manageable today might feel impossible tomorrow, depending on our resources, resilience, and overall stress load.

The Mind-Body Connection

One of the most fascinating aspects of stress is how it bridges the perceived gap between mind and body. When you experience stress, your body doesn't distinguish between physical and psychological threats—it responds with the same biological mechanisms whether you're facing a charging lion or an intimidating job interview.

This response begins in the brain. When you encounter a stressor:

1. Your amygdala (the brain's emotional processing center) recognizes a threat and signals the hypothalamus
2. The hypothalamus activates your sympathetic nervous system, triggering the "fight-or-flight" response
3. Your adrenal glands release stress hormones, including adrenaline and cortisol
4. These hormones create physical changes: increased heart rate and blood pressure, enhanced glucose availability, and redirected blood flow to muscles and vital organs

These changes are adaptive in the short term—they help you respond effectively to immediate threats. But when stress becomes chronic, this same system can wreak havoc on your health.

Recent research has revealed that chronic stress can:
- Suppress immune function, increasing susceptibility to infections and slowing healing
- Contribute to cardiovascular problems, including hypertension and increased risk of heart attack and stroke
- Disrupt sleep patterns, impairing cognitive function and emotional regulation
- Accelerate cellular aging through effects on telomeres (protective caps on chromosomes)
- Alter brain structure, particularly in areas involved in memory, learning, and emotional regulation
- Contribute to digestive issues, including irritable bowel syndrome and acid reflux
- Increase risk for mental health conditions, including anxiety and depression

The mind-body connection works in both directions. Just as mental stress creates physical effects, physical practices—like deep breathing, exercise, and adequate sleep—can reduce mental stress. This bidirectional relationship offers multiple pathways for effective stress management.

Reflection: What Does Stress Look Like in Your Life?

Take a moment to consider how stress manifests in your own experience. While some signs of stress are nearly universal, others are highly individual. Understanding your personal stress response is the first step toward effective management.

Consider these questions:
- **Physical signs**: Do you experience headaches, muscle tension, digestive issues, sleep disturbances, or changes in energy level when stressed?
- **Emotional indicators**: How does stress affect your mood? Do you become irritable, anxious, overwhelmed, or emotionally numb?
- **Cognitive impacts**: Does stress affect your thinking? Do you have trouble concentrating, making decisions, or remembering things?

- **Behavioral changes**: How does your behavior change under stress? Do you withdraw socially, increase use of substances, change eating patterns, or procrastinate more?

- **Stress triggers**: What situations, environments, or interactions most commonly trigger stress for you?

- **Stress responses**: What are your typical ways of responding to stress? Are they effective or do they create additional problems?

- **Eustress examples**: When have you experienced positive stress that energized and motivated you?

- **Distress examples**: When has stress felt overwhelming or harmful to your wellbeing?

Understanding your personal stress profile is not about judgment but awareness. By recognizing your unique stress patterns, you gain the power to respond more intentionally rather than react automatically.

As we continue through this book, you'll develop a comprehensive toolkit for transforming your relationship with stress—not eliminating it entirely (which would be neither possible nor desirable), but learning to harness its energy while minimizing its harmful effects. The journey from stressful to successful begins with this fundamental understanding: stress itself is neither inherently good nor bad. What matters is how we perceive, respond to, and recover from it.

Chapter 2: Mapping Your Unique Stress Profile

Everyone experiences stress, but no two people experience it exactly the same way. Your stress profile—the specific triggers that activate your stress response, the unique symptoms you experience, and your characteristic ways of responding—is as individual as your fingerprint. Understanding this personal stress signature is the first step toward transforming stress from an overwhelming force into a manageable, and even potentially beneficial, part of your life.

The Multi-Dimensional Nature of Stress

Stress operates on multiple levels simultaneously, affecting every aspect of your being:

Physical Stress includes illness, injury, environmental toxins, poor nutrition, inadequate sleep, excessive noise, and physical overexertion. Even positive physical activities like exercise create stress on the body, though in appropriate doses this stress stimulates growth and adaptation.

Psychological Stress encompasses emotional turmoil (anxiety, anger, grief), mental overload (information overwhelm, decision fatigue), and negative thought patterns (catastrophizing, perfectionism, rumination). The stories we tell ourselves about our experiences often generate more stress than the experiences themselves.

Psychosocial Stress involves relationship difficulties, workplace conflicts, financial pressures, caregiving responsibilities, and social isolation. As inherently social beings, our connections with others can be either our greatest source of support or our most significant stressor.

Psychospiritual Stress relates to crises of meaning, purpose, and values. When we live in ways that conflict with our core beliefs or when we struggle to find meaning in our experiences, we experience a deep form of stress that affects our entire being.

Understanding which dimensions of stress most affect you provides valuable insight into where to focus your stress management efforts.

Recognizing Your Stress Signals

Many people remain unaware of their stress levels until they reach a breaking point. Learning to recognize your early warning signs can help you intervene before stress becomes overwhelming.

Physical Signals

Your body often sends the first alerts that stress is building:

- **Sleep disturbances**: Difficulty falling asleep, staying asleep, or waking unrefreshed
- **Energy fluctuations**: Fatigue, restlessness, or both in alternation
- **Muscle tension**: Particularly in the neck, shoulders, jaw, and lower back
- **Digestive issues**: Appetite changes, stomach discomfort, constipation, or diarrhea
- **Immune changes**: Frequent minor illnesses or flare-ups of chronic conditions
- **Skin reactions**: Acne, eczema, psoriasis, or hives
- **Pain patterns**: Headaches, backaches, or generalized body aches
- **Cardiovascular signs**: Elevated heart rate, palpitations, or increased blood pressure

Psychological Signals

Your mental and emotional state offers important clues about your stress levels:

- **Mood changes**: Irritability, anxiety, sadness, or emotional numbness
- **Cognitive difficulties**: Trouble concentrating, memory lapses, or racing thoughts
- **Worry patterns**: Excessive concern about the future or rumination about the past
- **Decreased pleasure**: Reduced enjoyment in activities you typically find rewarding
- **Motivation shifts**: Procrastination, apathy, or conversely, hyperactivity
- **Perspective narrowing**: Catastrophizing or inability to see solutions

Behavioral Signals

How you act when stressed provides additional insights:

- **Relationship changes**: Withdrawal from others or increased conflict

- **Coping behaviors**: Increased use of substances, food, shopping, or screen time
- **Productivity shifts**: Overworking or underperforming
- **Time management issues**: Chronic lateness, rushing, or difficulty prioritizing
- **Self-care changes**: Neglecting basic needs like nutrition, hydration, or hygiene
- **Communication patterns**: Speaking more rapidly, interrupting, or becoming quieter

Identifying Your Stress Triggers

Stress triggers are the specific situations, interactions, or conditions that activate your stress response. While some triggers are universal (physical danger, major life changes), many are highly individual, shaped by your personality, past experiences, and current circumstances.

Common external triggers include:
- Work demands and deadlines
- Financial pressures
- Relationship conflicts
- Major life transitions
- Environmental factors (noise, crowding, etc.)
- News and social media exposure
- Time pressures and scheduling conflicts

Internal triggers can be even more powerful:
- Perfectionism and self-criticism
- Uncertainty or ambiguity
- Perceived lack of control
- Fear of failure or judgment
- Unresolved emotional issues

- Misalignment with personal values
- Negative thought patterns

Self-Assessment Exercise:
Take a moment to reflect on your recent experiences of stress:
1. When did you last feel significantly stressed?
2. What was happening at that time?
3. What physical sensations did you notice?
4. What emotions and thoughts arose?
5. How did you behave in response?
6. What helped you feel better?

By examining these patterns over time, you can begin to identify your unique stress signature.

The Social Readjustment Rating Scale: A Modern Perspective

In the 1960s, psychiatrists Thomas Holmes and Richard Rahe developed the Social Readjustment Rating Scale (SRRS) to measure the impact of major life events on stress levels and illness susceptibility. Their research showed that accumulating significant life changes within a short period substantially increased the risk of stress-related illness.

While the original scale remains valuable, our understanding of stress has evolved, and modern life presents challenges the original researchers couldn't have anticipated. Below is an updated version of the scale that includes contemporary stressors:

Modern Social Readjustment Rating Scale

Rank	Life Event	Impact Value
1	Death of spouse/partner	100
2	Divorce/end of long-term relationship	73
3	Marital/relationship separation	65
4	Jail term or serious legal problems	63

Rank	Life Event	Impact Value
5	Death of close family member	63
6	Major personal injury or illness	53
7	Marriage/domestic partnership	50
8	Job loss or forced retirement	47
9	Relationship reconciliation	45
10	Retirement (planned)	45
11	Major change in health of family member	44
12	Pregnancy or causing pregnancy	40
13	Sexual difficulties	39
14	Addition to family (birth, adoption, elder moving in)	39
15	Major business or career change	39
16	Major change in financial state	38
17	Death of close friend	37
18	Change to different line of work	36
19	Major change in relationship dynamics	35
20	Taking on significant debt (mortgage, loan)	31
21	Foreclosure or major financial loss	30
22	Change in work responsibilities	29
23	Child leaving home	29

Rank	Life Event	Impact Value
24	Trouble with in-laws or extended family	29
25	Outstanding personal achievement	28
26	Partner begins or stops working	26
27	Beginning or ending formal education	26
28	Major change in living conditions	25
29	Revision of personal habits or identity	24
30	Troubles with work supervisor/management	23
31	Major change in work conditions or hours	20
32	Change in residence	20
33	Change in schools or educational environment	20
34	Major change in recreational activities	19
35	Change in religious activities	19
36	Change in social activities	18
37	Taking on moderate debt	17
38	Change in sleeping habits	16
39	Change in family gathering frequency	15
40	Change in eating habits	15
41	Vacation/planned travel	13
42	Major holiday season	12

Rank	Life Event	Impact Value
43	Minor violations of the law	11
44	Ongoing social media conflicts	14
45	Persistent technology problems	14
46	Identity theft or privacy breach	30
47	Significant political/social upheaval	25
48	Pandemic or public health crisis	28
49	Climate-related disasters or concerns	22
50	Major home repairs or renovations	21

How to Use the Scale:

1. Add up the impact values for all events you've experienced in the past 12 months.

2. Interpret your score:

- Less than 150: Low susceptibility to stress-induced health breakdown

- 150-299: Moderate susceptibility (about 50% chance of serious health change)

- 300 or more: High susceptibility (about 80% chance of health breakdown)

Important Considerations:

- This scale measures major life changes, not daily hassles, which can also significantly impact stress levels.

- Individual responses to these events vary greatly based on personality, coping resources, and social support.

- The scale should be used as a general guideline, not a precise predictor of health outcomes.

- Even positive events (marriage, outstanding achievement) create stress through the demand for adaptation.

Your Unique Stress Response Pattern

When faced with stress, people tend to adopt characteristic response patterns. Understanding your typical responses can help you develop more effective coping strategies.

Common stress response patterns include:

Fight: Becoming confrontational, aggressive, or overly controlling when stressed.

- Signs: Anger, irritability, argumentativeness, blaming others
- Potential benefits: Energized to tackle problems directly
- Potential drawbacks: Relationship damage, impulsive decisions

Flight: Avoiding, escaping, or withdrawing from stressful situations.

- Signs: Procrastination, physical avoidance, excessive busyness
- Potential benefits: Creates space for emotional processing
- Potential drawbacks: Problems remain unaddressed, isolation

Freeze: Becoming immobilized or shutting down when stressed.

- Signs: Indecision, numbness, mental blankness, procrastination
- Potential benefits: Prevents hasty reactions
- Potential drawbacks: Inaction when action is needed

Fawn: Attempting to please others and avoid conflict when stressed.

- Signs: Excessive people-pleasing, difficulty setting boundaries
- Potential benefits: Maintains relationships during stress
- Potential drawbacks: Neglect of personal needs, resentment

Flow: Engaging with stress in a balanced, adaptive way.

- Signs: Staying present, maintaining perspective, appropriate action
- Potential benefits: Effective problem-solving, growth opportunity

- Potential drawbacks: Requires practice and self-awareness

Most people use a combination of these responses depending on the situation, but many have a dominant pattern they default to under pressure.

Journaling Prompt: Your Top 3 Stressors and How You React

Journaling is a powerful tool for understanding your stress patterns and developing greater self-awareness. Take some time to reflect on and write about the following:

Identify your top three current stressors:
1. What are the three situations, relationships, or circumstances causing you the most stress right now?
2. For each stressor, describe it in detail. What exactly about this situation triggers your stress response?
3. How long has each stressor been present in your life? Is it acute (temporary) or chronic (ongoing)?

Examine your reactions to each stressor:
1. Physical reactions: What happens in your body when you encounter this stressor?
2. Emotional reactions: What feelings arise? How intense are they?
3. Mental reactions: What thoughts or beliefs come up? Do you notice any thought patterns?
4. Behavioral reactions: What do you do in response to this stressor? How do you cope?

Explore the effectiveness of your responses:
1. How well do your current responses work for you?
2. What are the short-term and long-term consequences of how you typically respond?
3. What alternative responses might be more effective?

Consider your resources and support:
1. What internal resources (skills, strengths, perspectives) help you manage this stressor?

2. What external resources (people, tools, environments) support you?
3. What additional resources might help you respond more effectively?

Sample Journaling Format:

Stressor #1: [Describe the stressor]

- Physical reactions:
- Emotional reactions:
- Mental reactions:
- Behavioral reactions:
- Effectiveness of my response:
- Alternative approaches:
- Resources that help:
- Additional resources I need:

[Repeat for Stressors #2 and #3]

Regular journaling about your stress experiences can reveal patterns you might not otherwise notice and provide valuable insights for developing your personalized stress management approach.

Summary

Understanding your unique stress profile—your specific triggers, symptoms, and response patterns—is the foundation for effective stress management. By becoming more aware of how stress manifests in your life, you gain the power to intervene earlier and more effectively.

Remember that stress itself is not the enemy. Rather, it's unrecognized, unmanaged, and chronic stress that poses the greatest threat to your wellbeing. With greater self-awareness and appropriate tools, you can transform your relationship with stress from one of helpless reactivity to one of empowered response.

In the next chapter, we'll explore the hidden costs of chronic stress and how it affects various aspects of your health and well-being. This understanding will further motivate your journey from stressful to successful.

Chapter 3: The Hidden Costs of Stress

Stress is often described as an inevitable part of modern life, but its true costs run deeper than most people realize. While short bursts of stress can motivate and focus us, chronic or poorly managed stress can undermine our health, strain our relationships, sap our productivity, and erode our sense of meaning and purpose. Understanding these hidden costs is the first step toward transforming stress from a destructive force into a catalyst for positive change.

The Toll on Health

Chronic stress is a major contributor to a wide range of health problems. It is estimated that up to 70–80% of all visits to primary care physicians are related to stress or stress-induced conditions. Prolonged activation of the body's stress response system can lead to:

- **Cardiovascular disease:** Stress increases blood pressure, heart rate, and the risk of arrhythmias and heart attacks. Studies show that people with little control over their work environment are at higher risk for heart disease, while those who thrive on challenge and autonomy may be less affected.

- **Immune suppression:** Stress suppresses immune function, increasing susceptibility to infections, allergies, and even cancer. For example, people under significant stress are more likely to catch colds and experience slower recovery from illness.

- **Metabolic and endocrine disruption:** Chronic stress can contribute to diabetes, hormonal imbalances, and digestive problems such as irritable bowel syndrome and ulcers.

- **Mental health disorders:** Anxiety, depression, insomnia, and mood swings are all linked to ongoing stress. Personality type also plays a role—those with "Type A" personalities (competitive, driven, impatient) are more prone to stress-related illnesses than their more relaxed "Type B" counterparts.

Case Study: June, a 30-year-old sales representative and mother of two, suffered from fatigue, mood swings, and frequent illness. After a comprehensive assessment, her naturopathic physician found that a combination of physical and emotional stressors, poor diet, and adrenal fatigue were undermining her health. Through dietary changes, nutritional supplements, herbal support, and daily relaxation practices, June regained much of her energy and resilience within a year.

Impact on Relationships

Stress rarely stays contained within us; it spills over into our interactions with others. When we are stressed, we are more likely to:

- Withdraw from loved ones or become irritable and short-tempered
- Struggle to communicate effectively, leading to misunderstandings and conflict
- Neglect important relationships due to time pressures or emotional exhaustion
- Rely on negative coping mechanisms (such as substance use or overeating), which can further strain relationships

Healthy relationships are a vital buffer against stress, but they require attention and care. As highlighted in the *About Things That Matter* series, the quality of our relationships is a key pillar of lasting success and well-being.

Case Study: A 52-year-old lawyer working long hours developed headaches, insomnia, and high blood pressure. With support from a traditional Chinese medicine practitioner, including acupuncture, herbs, and Qigong exercises, he not only improved his physical health but also learned to set boundaries and reconnect with his family, reducing both his stress and its relational fallout.

Productivity and Performance

While some stress can sharpen focus and drive, chronic stress undermines our ability to perform at our best. The hidden costs include:

- **Reduced concentration and memory:** Stress impairs cognitive function, making it harder to focus, solve problems, or make decisions.
- **Increased absenteeism and presenteeism:** People under chronic stress are more likely to miss work or be less effective when present.
- **Burnout:** Persistent stress without adequate recovery leads to emotional exhaustion, cynicism, and a sense of ineffectiveness.
- **Higher rates of errors and accidents:** Studies show that stressed workers are more prone to mistakes and injuries, particularly in high-stakes or high-pressure environments.

Case Study: Air traffic controllers with "Type A" personalities experienced more job-related injuries and illnesses than their "Type B" colleagues, highlighting the impact of stress on workplace safety and performance.

Erosion of Meaning and Purpose

Perhaps the most insidious cost of stress is its ability to sap our sense of meaning and fulfillment. Chronic stress can:

- Narrow our focus to immediate survival, crowding out long-term goals and aspirations
- Lead to a sense of helplessness, hopelessness, or loss of direction
- Undermine our motivation and joy, even in activities we once loved

As discussed in the *About Things That Matter* series, true success is not measured solely by wealth or achievement but by our ability to pursue the things that matter most—relationships, health, personal growth, and purpose. When stress dominates our lives, these deeper sources of meaning can be neglected or forgotten.

The Opportunity: Transforming Stress into Growth

The good news is that stress, when recognized and managed effectively, can become a powerful catalyst for positive change. Many people discover new strengths, clarify their values, and build resilience in the face of adversity. The key is not to eliminate stress entirely—an impossible and undesirable goal—but to develop the awareness and skills needed to respond to stress constructively.

Key Strategies:

- **Awareness:** Notice your stress signals early and identify their sources.
- **Connection:** Reach out for support and invest in relationships that matter.
- **Self-care:** Prioritize sleep, nutrition, movement, and relaxation.
- **Meaning:** Reconnect with your values and purpose, using stress as a signal to realign your life.

Case Study: After losing her job, Maria, a mid-career professional, initially experienced anxiety and self-doubt. Through journaling, support from friends, and a renewed focus on her core values, she used the crisis as an opportunity to pursue a more meaningful career path and deepen her relationships.

Reflection

- In what ways has stress affected your health, relationships, productivity, or sense of meaning?

- Can you identify a time when stress prompted you to make a positive change?

- What support or resources might help you transform current stressors into opportunities for growth?

Summary: The hidden costs of stress are real and far-reaching, but they are not inevitable. By understanding how stress impacts every dimension of life—and by choosing to respond with awareness, connection, and purpose—you can turn stress from a hidden saboteur into a source of strength and transformation.

The Science of Resilience and Growth

Chapter 4: How Stress Can Help You Grow

Neuroplasticity and Building Resilience

For decades, stress was seen primarily as a health hazard. Recent research, however, reveals a more nuanced truth: stress, when understood and managed well, can be a catalyst for growth and positive change. This is possible because of **neuroplasticity**—the brain's remarkable ability to reorganize itself by forming new neural connections throughout life. When you encounter stress and respond with adaptive strategies, your brain literally rewires itself, strengthening pathways that support resilience, problem-solving, and emotional regulation.

Resilience—the capacity to bounce back from adversity—is not a fixed trait. It can be developed through repeated practice, much like a muscle. Each time you face a challenge and respond with awareness and constructive action, you build your resilience "muscle," making it easier to handle future stressors.

The Role of Mindset (Growth vs. Fixed)

Your mindset—the beliefs you hold about your abilities and potential—plays a critical role in how you respond to stress. Psychologist Carol Dweck's research distinguishes between a **fixed mindset** (believing abilities are static) and a **growth mindset** (believing abilities can be developed through effort and learning).

- **Fixed mindset:** "I'm just not good at handling pressure."
- **Growth mindset:** "I can learn strategies to manage stress better."

Those who approach stress with a growth mindset are more likely to see challenges as opportunities for learning and self-improvement, rather than threats to be avoided. This shift in perspective transforms stress from a purely negative experience into a driver of personal development.

Stories of Transformation: Stress-to-Success Journeys

Case 1: Career Change under Pressure

After being laid off unexpectedly, Maria initially spiraled into anxiety and self-doubt. Instead of retreating, she used the opportunity to reflect on her values and passions. Through journaling and support from friends, Maria retrained for a new career in a field that aligned with her interests. Today, she credits the stressful event as the turning point that led her to a more meaningful and fulfilling path.

Case 2: Health Crisis as a Catalyst

James, a mid-level manager, suffered a heart attack brought on by chronic workplace stress. During recovery, he adopted mindfulness practices and regular exercise, and re-evaluated his work-life balance. Not only did his health improve, but his relationships deepened and he discovered a renewed sense of purpose.

Case 3: Academic Pressure and Mindset Shift

Lina, a university student, faced overwhelming pressure to achieve top grades. Initially, she viewed setbacks as proof she "wasn't cut out" for her program. After learning about growth mindset, she reframed failures as feedback and focused on learning rather than perfection. Her academic performance improved, but more importantly, her confidence and resilience flourished.

Key Insight: Stressful experiences, when met with self-awareness and a willingness to grow, can become the very soil in which resilience, wisdom, and success take root.

Chapter 5: The Four Pathways to Success

There is no single formula for turning stress into success, but research and lived experience point to four essential pathways: Awareness, Acceptance, Action, and Achievement. Each builds upon the last, creating a sustainable framework for growth.

1. Awareness: Noticing Your Stress Patterns

Change begins with awareness. This means paying attention to your unique stress triggers, symptoms, and habitual responses—without judgment. Self-awareness allows you to catch stress early, identify patterns, and make conscious choices rather than reacting automatically.

Practice:
- Keep a stress journal to track triggers and responses.
- Use mindfulness techniques to observe thoughts and bodily sensations.

2. Acceptance: Making Peace with Imperfection

Many people waste precious energy fighting against reality or wishing circumstances were different. Acceptance is not resignation; it's the willingness to acknowledge what is, including your own imperfections and limitations. This creates space for compassion, patience, and realistic expectations.

Practice:
- Practice self-compassion and acknowledge that setbacks are part of growth.
- Use affirmations such as, "It's okay to feel stressed sometimes; I am learning and growing."

3. Action: Small Steps, Big Changes (Kaizen Principle)

Lasting change rarely comes from dramatic overhauls. Instead, the Japanese principle of **Kaizen**—continuous improvement through small, consistent steps—offers a sustainable path forward. By breaking goals into manageable actions, you reduce overwhelm and build momentum.

Practice:
- Identify one small, positive change you can make today (e.g., 5 minutes of deep breathing, a short walk, or a single conversation).
- Track your progress and celebrate each step, no matter how minor.

4. Achievement: Redefining and Celebrating Success

Achievement is not just about reaching a final goal, but about recognizing progress and growth along the way. Redefine success in terms of what truly matters to you—not society's expectations. Celebrate milestones, however small, and use them as motivation to continue your journey.

Practice:
- Reflect regularly on your progress and what you've learned.
- Share your successes with supportive friends or mentors.
- Create rituals or rewards that honor your achievements.

In Summary: Resilience is not the absence of stress, but the ability to engage with stress in ways that foster growth, learning, and fulfillment. By cultivating awareness, acceptance, action, and achievement, you transform stress from a stumbling block into a stepping stone on your path to success.

Building Your Personalized Success Blueprint

Chapter 6: Calming the Mind and Body

Stress management begins with learning to calm both the mind and body. Modern science and ancient wisdom agree: when you activate the body's relaxation response, you counteract the harmful effects of chronic stress and build a foundation for resilience and growth.

Updated Relaxation Techniques

1. **Breathwork.** Diaphragmatic breathing (or "belly breathing") is a cornerstone of stress reduction. By focusing on slow, deep breaths that expand the abdomen, you signal your nervous system to shift from "fight or flight" to "rest and digest." Try the 4-7-8 technique: inhale for 4 seconds, hold for 7, exhale for 8.

2. **Mindfulness.** Mindfulness is the practice of paying attention to the present moment without judgment. Research shows it reduces anxiety, improves focus, and fosters emotional regulation. Start with five minutes a day, simply noticing your breath, sensations, or thoughts as they come and go.

3. **Guided Imagery.** This technique uses the imagination to create calming mental images. Picture yourself in a peaceful place—a beach, forest, or favorite room. Engage all your senses: What do you see, hear, feel, or smell? Guided imagery can be practiced solo or with the help of recordings.

4. **Yoga.** Yoga integrates movement, breath, and mindfulness. Regular practice has been shown to lower cortisol, reduce muscle tension, and improve mood. Choose a style and level that suits your needs—from gentle restorative yoga to more active vinyasa flows.

Digital Tools: Apps, Audio Guides, and Online Resources

- **Meditation apps:** Calm, Headspace, Insight Timer, and Smiling Mind offer guided meditations, breathwork, and sleep stories.

- **Yoga platforms:** Yoga with Adriene (YouTube), Glo, and Down Dog provide classes for all levels.

- **Biofeedback devices:** Tools like HeartMath and Muse offer real-time feedback on your physiological state, helping you learn to self-regulate.

- **Podcasts and audio guides:** Search for mindfulness, relaxation, or sleep podcasts for on-the-go support.

Reflection: Which Techniques Resonate With You?

Not every technique works for everyone. Experiment with several methods and notice which ones help you feel calm, centered, and recharged. Ask yourself:

- Which practice feels most natural or enjoyable?
- When do you notice the greatest benefit—morning, midday, or evening?
- Are there digital resources that make it easier for you to stay consistent?

Write down your observations and commit to practicing your chosen technique(s) daily, even if only for a few minutes.

Chapter 7: Designing a Supportive Lifestyle

A resilient, successful life is built on daily habits and supportive routines. The way you manage your time, relationships, movement, and rest all contribute to your ability to handle stress and thrive.

Time Management for Modern Life

- **Prioritize:** Identify your most important tasks each day and focus your energy there.
- **Set boundaries:** Learn to say "no" to commitments that don't align with your goals or values.
- **Break tasks into steps:** Use lists, planners, or apps to organize your day into manageable pieces.
- **Avoid multitasking:** Focus on one thing at a time for greater efficiency and less overwhelm.

Building Healthy Relationships and Boundaries

- **Communicate openly:** Express your needs and listen actively to others.
- **Nurture supportive connections:** Invest time in relationships that uplift and energize you.
- **Set boundaries:** Protect your time and energy by clearly defining what is and isn't acceptable.
- **Seek support:** Don't hesitate to ask for help or lean on your network during challenging times.

Exercise as Joy, Not Obligation

- **Find movement you enjoy:** Walking, dancing, cycling, swimming, yoga, or team sports can all be effective.
- **Make it social:** Exercise with friends or family for added motivation and connection.
- **Listen to your body:** Aim for consistency, not intensity. Even short, gentle sessions are beneficial.

Sleep, Rest, and Digital Detox

- **Prioritize sleep:** Aim for 7–9 hours per night, keeping a consistent bedtime and wake time.

- **Create restful routines:** Wind down with calming activities—reading, stretching, or meditation.

- **Limit screen time:** Take regular breaks from devices, especially before bed, to support deep rest.

Action Plan: Your Lifestyle Audit

Take stock of your current routines:

- Where are your biggest sources of support?

- Where do you feel most depleted or overwhelmed?

- What is one small change you can make this week to support your well-being?

Write down your answers and revisit them regularly to track your progress and adjust as needed.

Chapter 8: Eating for Energy and Resilience

Nutrition is a powerful tool for managing stress and supporting overall resilience. The right foods can stabilize mood, boost energy, and help your body recover from daily challenges.

Nutrition for Stress Management: What's New

- **Whole foods focus:** Prioritize fruits, vegetables, whole grains, lean proteins, and healthy fats.
- **Balance blood sugar:** Eat regular meals and snacks to avoid energy crashes and mood swings.
- **Limit stimulants:** Reduce caffeine and sugar, which can exacerbate anxiety and disrupt sleep.
- **Hydration:** Drink plenty of water throughout the day.

Meal Planning for Busy Lives

- **Prep ahead:** Batch-cook meals or prep ingredients in advance.
- **Simple recipes:** Choose quick, nutritious meals that fit your schedule.
- **Healthy snacks:** Keep nuts, seeds, fruit, and yogurt on hand for easy, nourishing options.

Addressing Food Sensitivities and Allergies

- **Notice patterns:** Track symptoms after meals to identify potential triggers.
- **Consult professionals:** Work with a healthcare provider or dietitian if you suspect sensitivities.
- **Elimination diets:** Consider short-term elimination of common allergens (e.g., gluten, dairy, soy) to test for improvement.

Mindful Eating Practices

- **Eat slowly:** Savor each bite and pay attention to hunger and fullness cues.
- **Minimize distractions:** Avoid screens and multitasking during meals.
- **Gratitude:** Take a moment to appreciate your food and those who made it possible.

Worksheet: Your Stress-Resilient Meal Plan
- List your favorite nourishing breakfasts, lunches, dinners, and snacks.
- Identify one area for improvement (e.g., more vegetables, less sugar).
- Plan your meals for the week, including shopping and prep time.
- Reflect on how your eating habits affect your energy and mood.

Chapter 9: Supplements and Herbal Allies

When stress is high or nutrition is lacking, supplements and herbs can provide additional support. Always consult with a healthcare provider before starting new supplements, especially if you have health conditions or take medication.

Evidence-Based Review of Key Nutrients and Adaptogens

- **Vitamin C:** Supports adrenal function and immune health.
- **B vitamins:** Essential for energy production and nervous system balance.
- **Magnesium:** Calms the nervous system and reduces muscle tension.
- **Zinc:** Important for immune resilience and mood regulation.
- **Adaptogens:** Herbs like ginseng (Panax and Siberian), ashwagandha, rhodiola, and holy basil help the body adapt to stress and restore balance.

Safety, Sourcing, and Integration with Medical Care

- **Quality matters:** Choose reputable brands and check for third-party testing.
- **Start low, go slow:** Begin with lower doses and monitor for side effects.
- **Integrate, don't replace:** Supplements should complement—not substitute—healthy diet and lifestyle practices.
- **Medical supervision:** Always inform your healthcare provider of any supplements or herbs you are taking.

Case Examples: Integrative Approaches

- **Case 1:** A busy professional with chronic fatigue benefits from magnesium and B-complex supplementation, along with regular yoga and mindful eating.
- **Case 2:** A parent struggling with anxiety finds relief through ashwagandha, guided imagery, and improved sleep hygiene.
- **Case 3:** An older adult with immune challenges uses vitamin C, zinc, and gentle exercise to boost resilience during high-stress periods.

Summary: Building your personalized success blueprint means integrating calming practices, supportive routines, nourishing foods, and targeted supplements into your daily life. By making small, consistent changes, you lay the groundwork for lasting resilience and well-being.

From Surviving to Thriving

Chapter 10: Mastering Your Mindset

A resilient, successful life begins in the mind. While stress is inevitable, how you interpret and respond to it is shaped by your mindset. Mastering your mindset means moving beyond negative coping patterns, building habits of optimism and gratitude, and rewriting your personal stress story.

Overcoming Negative Coping Patterns

Negative coping patterns—like avoidance, denial, substance use, or self-criticism—may offer short-term relief but ultimately reinforce stress and undermine well-being1. The first step is to identify your default responses under pressure. Are you prone to rumination, procrastination, or blaming yourself or others? Awareness is the foundation for change.

Replace negative patterns with constructive strategies:

- Practice self-reflection and name your feelings.

- Use relaxation techniques (breathwork, mindfulness, exercise) to interrupt stress cycles.

- Seek support or professional help when needed.

Building Optimism, Gratitude, and Self-Compassion

Optimism is not blind positivity; it's the belief that you can influence outcomes and recover from setbacks. Research shows that optimistic people experience less distress and better health outcomes. Cultivate optimism by:

- Challenging catastrophic thoughts and reframing setbacks as temporary or solvable.

- Keeping a gratitude journal—list three things you're thankful for each day.

- Practicing self-compassion: treat yourself with the same kindness you would offer a friend in difficulty.

Journaling: Rewriting Your Stress Story

Journaling can transform your relationship with stress. Use these prompts to rewrite your narrative:

- Recall a recent stressful event. What was your initial reaction? How did you cope?

- What strengths or resources did you use, even if the outcome wasn't perfect?

- How might you view the situation differently with a growth mindset?
- What would you say to a friend in your shoes?

By regularly reflecting and rewriting your story, you reinforce resilience and open the door to new possibilities.

Chapter 11: Habits That Matter

Habits are the building blocks of lasting change. Small, consistent actions—especially when "stacked" onto existing routines—can dramatically increase your stress resilience and sense of control.

Habit Stacking and Micro-Habits for Stress Resilience

- **Habit stacking**: Attach a new, positive habit to an established one (e.g., practice three deep breaths after brushing your teeth).

- **Micro-habits**: Choose actions so small they're almost effortless (e.g., one-minute gratitude reflection, a single stretch, or a glass of water upon waking).

These incremental changes are sustainable and reduce overwhelm.

Using Kaizen for Continuous Improvement

The Kaizen principle—continuous improvement through small steps—applies to stress management as well. Rather than aiming for perfection, focus on progress:

- Identify one small area to improve each week.

- Celebrate each success, no matter how minor.

- Adjust and iterate as you learn what works best for you.

Tracking Progress: Templates and Tools

- Use habit trackers (apps or paper) to monitor your consistency.

- Set weekly or monthly check-ins to review what's working and where you're struggling.

- Reflect on setbacks as opportunities for learning, not failures.

With time, these habits become automatic, forming a strong foundation for resilience and thriving.

Chapter 12: The Power of Connection

Humans are wired for connection. Social support is one of the most powerful buffers against stress and a crucial ingredient for thriving.

Community, Support Networks, and Seeking Help

- **Community**: Join groups, clubs, or activities that align with your interests and values.

- **Support networks**: Nurture relationships with friends, family, mentors, or colleagues who offer understanding and encouragement.

- **Seeking help**: Don't hesitate to reach out for professional support (counseling, coaching, support groups) when needed.

Communication Skills for Reducing Relational Stress

- Practice active listening: focus fully on the other person, reflect back what you hear, and avoid interrupting.

- Express your needs and feelings clearly and respectfully.

- Set healthy boundaries and be willing to say "no" when necessary.

Effective communication reduces misunderstandings and builds trust, making it easier to navigate conflict and change.

Reflection: Who's On Your Team?

Take a moment to map your support system:

- Who can you turn to for emotional support, practical help, or honest feedback?

- Are there relationships you'd like to strengthen or repair?

- What new connections might you seek to expand your circle of support?

Remember, thriving is not a solo journey. The power of connection transforms stress into shared strength and opens the door to greater fulfillment and success.

Summary: Thriving beyond stress is possible when you master your mindset, build supportive habits, and invest in meaningful connections. Each step moves you from mere survival toward a life of purpose, resilience, and joy.

Part 5
SUSTAINING SUCCESS

Chapter 13: Navigating Setbacks and Change

Stress as Part of Growth and Transformation

Change and setbacks are inevitable on any journey toward success. Rather than seeing stress as a sign of failure or weakness, recognize it as a natural part of growth and transformation. Each challenge is an opportunity to build your resilience, refine your strategies, and clarify your values.

Emotional Agility and Bouncing Back

Emotional agility means being able to acknowledge your feelings—especially the difficult ones—without getting stuck in them. When setbacks occur, practice:

- Naming and accepting your emotions without judgment.
- Reflecting on what the experience is teaching you.
- Adjusting your plans, not abandoning your goals.

Resilience isn't about never falling; it's about rising each time you do, a little wiser and stronger.

Series Tie-In: Embracing Change as a Core Value

The *About Things That Matter* series emphasizes embracing change as a foundation for growth. Just as you learned to set purposeful goals and manage your time, learning to navigate change with flexibility and courage is a core life skill. Every setback can be reframed as a step forward in your personal evolution.

Chapter 14: Celebrating Progress, Not Perfection

Recognizing Wins, Big and Small

Sustained success is built on the recognition of all progress—not just major milestones, but every small step forward. Celebrate:

- Daily habits kept
- New skills learned
- Improved relationships
- Healthier responses to stress

Rituals for Self-Renewal

Create rituals that honor your journey and replenish your energy. This could be a weekly reflection, a gratitude practice, a walk in nature, or a special meal with loved ones. Rituals anchor your progress and provide moments of joy and rest.

Your Ongoing Journey: Resources for the Road Ahead

Success is not a destination but a lifelong process. Continue to invest in your growth by:

- Seeking out new learning opportunities
- Connecting with supportive communities
- Revisiting your vision and goals regularly
- Using setbacks as feedback, not failure

Conclusion: Living a Life That Matters

Integrating Stress Management into Your Purpose and Values

Stress management is not just about reducing discomfort—it's about creating the internal conditions that allow you to live in alignment with your deepest values and purpose. When you use stress as a signal for needed change, you transform it from a barrier into a bridge to a more meaningful life.

Invitation to Continue with Other About Things That Matter Books

This book is part of a larger journey. The *About Things That Matter* series offers further tools and insights for living with intention, setting and achieving purposeful goals, and building habits that support your best self. Explore the other books in the series to deepen your growth and sustain your success.

Final Reflection: What Does "Successful" Mean to You Now?

Take a moment to reflect:

- How has your definition of success changed through this process?
- What matters most to you now?
- How will you continue to honor your journey from stressful to successful?

Bibliography

Major Research Foundations Referenced

- Harvard's Grant Study – 80-year longitudinal study on human flourishing

- Stanford University research – Growth mindset and achievement, notably work by Dr. Carol Dweck

- MIT – Studies on habit formation and behavioral change

- Organizational psychology research – high-performance teamwork and support

Your Gift

As a way of saying thanks for your purchase, I'm offering you the first book in the series **About Things That Matter** as a gift.

This book is exclusive to my readers. You will not find this book anywhere else.

You're invited to pause, reflect, and reconsider what truly defines a meaningful life. In a world conditioned to chase money, status, and material achievements, this book challenges the conventional yardsticks of success. Through incisive insight and refreshing authenticity, it guides readers to shift their focus from external validation to the internal foundations that cultivate real fulfillment, purpose, and enduring happiness. It's a call to eliminate distractions, clarify values, and build a life anchored in what matters most.

Visit this link to download your free copy of [About Things That Matter](https://BookHip.com/HLAJBFP) or type this address into your browser https://BookHip.com/HLAJBFP

About JC Ryan

JC Ryan is a bestselling author renowned for his intricate espionage, archaeological thrillers, and conspiracy mysteries. With over 30 acclaimed novels, including the popular Rex Dalton K9 Thrillers, Rossler Foundation Mysteries, and Carter Devereux Mystery Thrillers, Ryan has captivated readers around the globe.

Drawing from his diverse professional background—as a military officer, lawyer, and IT manager—Ryan creates compelling narratives that skillfully blend historical accuracy with thrilling adventure. He is celebrated as a master storyteller, known for crafting riveting plots, meticulous historical details, and engaging, multidimensional characters. Ryan's meticulous research lends authenticity and depth to each story, immersing readers in richly constructed worlds filled with intrigue, suspense, and adventure.

Fans of David Baldacci, Lee Child's Jack Reacher, Tom Clancy's Jack Ryan, Nelson DeMille's John Corey, Vince Flynn's Mitch Rapp, Mark Greaney's Gray Man, Gregg Hurwitz's Orphan X, Robert Ludlum's Jason Bourne, Daniel Silva's Gabriel Allon, Brad Taylor's Pike Logan, Brad Thor's Scot Harvath, James Rollins' Sigma Force, Steve Berry's Cotton Malone, and Dan Brown's Robert Langdon will find JC Ryan's novels equally compelling and unforgettable.

When not writing, Ryan enjoys spending time with his college sweetheart, whom he married in 1978. They are proud parents of two daughters, have two sons-in-law, and are grandparents to two grandchildren.

Also by JC Ryan

Rex Dalton K9 Thrillers

Here's what readers are saying about the series:

"A great read, started and couldn't stop until the end!!!"

"Just gets better and better. Can't wait to read the next in the series."

"Rex and Digger return. The continuing story of Rex Dalton and Digger is a suspenseful and intriguing work."

"What's A Dog To Do? 5 stars. I love reading about Rex Dalton's exploits, but my favorite character has to be Digger, his military-trained super-intelligent dog."

"JC Ryan scores again. I was not a fan of the first Rex Dalton book, but I plunged ahead with the second, hoping JC Ryan would not disappoint. I loved it. Now here I am after reading the third book in this series. I had a hard time putting it down and found myself wondering about it when I was not reading. Rex has added several new ports of call to this adventure. He sure gets into more trouble than any person I know who just wants to become a sightseer. With the help of Digger (his new comrade-in-arms), we are once again trying to correct the wrongs inflicted on the weak."

Visit The Rex Dalton Series Page http://viewbook.at/RexDaltonSeries

The Rossler Foundation Mysteries

http://myBook.to/RosslerFoundation

Here's what readers are saying about the series:

"A brilliant series by a master of the techno thrillers turning old much debated mysteries into overwhelming modern engrossing sagas of adventure, heroism and a sense of awe for the many mysteries still unexplained in our universe. Enjoy!"

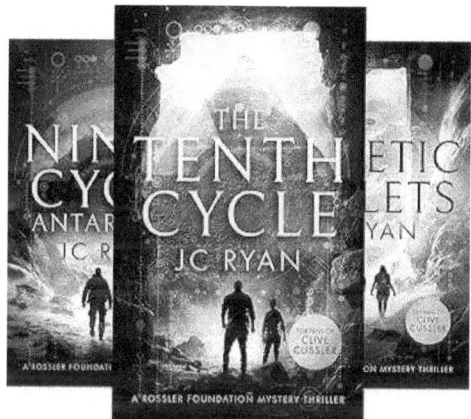

"I LOVED this series! It's readily apparent that the author drew from a large body of knowledge in writing this series. It's just believable enough to think it could happen someday, and in fact, aligns quite well with some of the current relationships that exist between present-day countries and the USA."

The Carter Devereux Mystery Thrillers

myBook.to/CarterDevereux

Here's what readers are saying about the series:

"Omg, this series is awesome. Full of adventure, action, romance, and suspense. If you start reading, you are hooked. Carter and all characters are awesome, you will fall in love with all of them they become like family. I love the way J C weaves the human and animals together in the story. Try it you will love it."

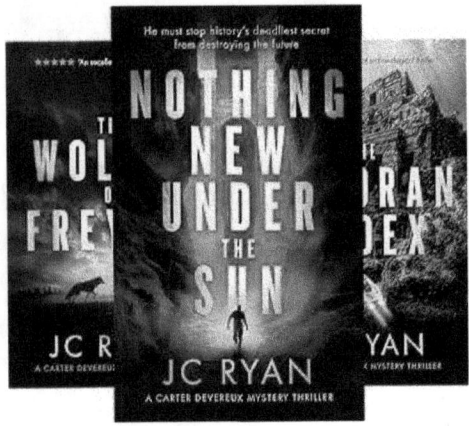

"The best! What a joy to read these four books about Carter and Mackenzie Devereux and their adventures. A very good read. I will look for more of JC Ryan's books."

"Suspenseful! Fabulous just fabulous! I enjoyed reading these books immensely. I highly recommend these books. Bravo to the author! You won't regret it."

"What a wonderful and intriguing book. Kept me glued to what was going to happen next. Not a normal read for me. But a very enjoyable series that I would recommend to everyone who likes adventure and thrills."

Satire and Humor

https://mybook.to/SnarkFiles

In a world where words are outlawed, news is tranquilized, and history is bubble-wrapped, The Snark Files dares to ask the questions everyone else is too comfortable to touch. Each file is a darkly comic record of society's most absurd attempts to outlaw reality, rebrand common sense, and algorithm-proof the obvious.

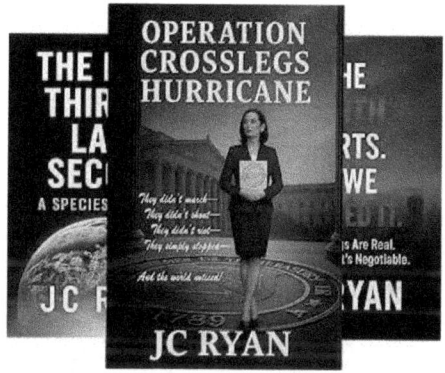

From professors fired for quoting Aristotle, to news anchors forced to deliver "comfort reports," to bureaucrats panicking over a lost Manual of Common Sense, the series exposes the hilarious fragility of a culture addicted to feelings, euphemisms, and spin.

Wry, biting, and disturbingly plausible, The Snark Files read like classified documents accidentally left on the copier—records of a civilization so desperate to protect itself from offense that it banned the very tools of truth.

Think Orwell with a laugh track. Swift with Wi-Fi. Douglas Adams at a government hearing.

If you've ever wondered how far nonsense can go before it collapses under its own contradictions, this is your front-row seat.

www.ingramcontent.com/pod-product-compliance
Lightning Source LLC
Chambersburg PA
CBHW080540030426

42337CB00024B/4806